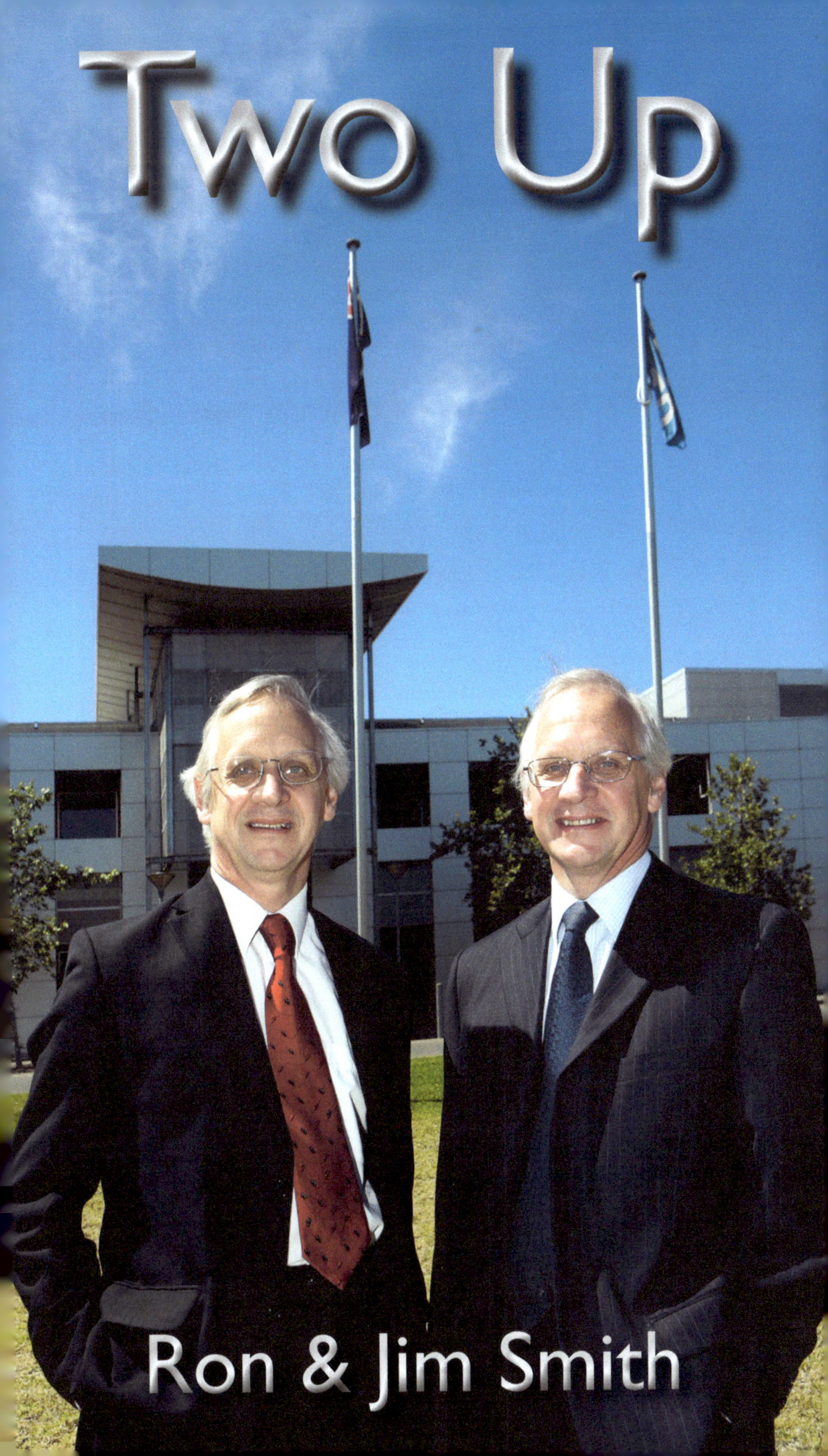
Two Up
Ron & Jim Smith

First published in 2014 by U P Publications under ISBN 978-1908135384
Second Edition published in Great Britain in 2017 by U P Publications
St George's House, George Street, Huntingdon, Cambridgeshire, UK PE29 3GH. UK

Front Picture copyright © Defence Science & Technology Organisation (DSTO)
(with permission) 2013
Cover Design copyright © U P Publications 2013, 2017

A CIP Catalogue record of this book is available from the British Library

ISBN 978-1908135391

SECOND EDITION

9 5 7 0 8 1 6 4 2 3

Also published as an e-book by U P Publications

ISBN 978-1908135445

Published by U P Publications
Printed in England by The Lightning Source Group

www.ronandjimsmith.com

www.uppublications.ltd.uk

Two Up

By Ron & Jim Smith

2017

The T21 Sedbergh or 'Barge'
Kenley Aerodrome, Surrey, summer of 1967.

Part 1
All You need
is Lift

Jim Smith

Chapter One

"Turned a Whiter Shade of Pale"

Basic training gliders are not noted for their aerobatic capability. This tale describes a not entirely successful attempt and its consequences.

RAF Kenley had been one of the home defence airfields for London, and saw heavy action in the Battle of Britain. An airfield full of history, but at the time of this episode, a focus for the Air Training Corps, or the Air Cadets, as they are now known.

574 Sqn ATC was based at Caterham School, and my brother and I were both active members of the Squadron, through which, we had learned to drill (not very well), to shoot 0.22 and 0.303 rifles at targets (quite well) and to compete successfully at both swimming and cross-country running. We were now embarked on learning to fly gliders, which at 16 and still at school, was a thrill.

The gliders we flew were either the Slingsby T21 Sedbergh, or the Slingsby T31 Cadet Mk 3, otherwise known as a Tandem Tutor.

These gliders were launched on a cable, using a powerful winch, which would generally deliver a launch height of about 800 ft above the upwind end of the airfield.

It must be stressed that this was not the high-tech, carbon fibre, digitally instrumented gliding of today.

Both the Sedbergh and the Cadet had open cockpits and strut-braced high wings. They were made of wood, covered with silver-doped fabric and had a strong tendency to sink rather than to soar. As a result, the flying would perhaps consist of four 5-minute single circuits spread out through the whole of the day, with the rest of the day spent manoeuvring gliders around, helping to retrieve them, or signalling to the winch driver using a large DayGlo bat to indicate that the glider was ready to launch.

But one should not get the wrong impression.

The pace of the flying might not have been great, but this was the very first opportunity to control an aircraft in the air. To sit in the cockpit, giving the command 'Take up Slack', and waiting with tension increasing, just like the tension in the cable as the winch slowly straightened it out. Then 'All Out !' and the glider would leap forward, becoming airborne almost instantly.

This was indeed a thrill.

Aiming for maximum height from the winch launch

The climb on the winch was steep, and airspeed was kept quite low, at perhaps 45 kt. The cable had a 1000lb weak link, which actually meant plenty of tension was available to provide the necessary climb rate. As one neared the top of the climb, the glider would flatten out – this was the time to lower the nose to take tension off the cable, and pull the release, and float quietly off the top of the launch into what would almost invariably be a simple circuit back to land.

The two types of glider were similar in having low performance, but were actually somewhat different to fly. The Sedbergh had side-by-side seating, and was affectionately known as 'the Barge'. It really was capable of flight at extraordinarily low speeds. I distinctly remember floating along in one in later years, working the ridge at Nympsfield at an indicated airspeed of less than 30 kts. This was achieved by a magnificently thick and quite highly cambered wing, which delivered the extraordinary low-speed performance, but at the expense of high drag.

The Cadet was angular where the Sedbergh was curvaceous. It had tandem seats (with the instructor behind the student), a much thinner wing, braced by twin parallel struts each side, these in-turn being braced by wires. Compared to the Sedbergh, it seemed to me to have little to offer in the way of advantage.

True, it did tend to fly a little faster, probably because of a smaller wing area, but with extra struts and wires, and a more angular fuselage, it certainly came down just as fast. Additionally, it was a noisier aircraft, partly because of the wind noise from the wire bracing, but also because the instructor tended to shout - a lot.

Another abiding memory is just how painful ice crystals can be when striking one's unprotected face in the open cockpit of one of these gliders.

With the hindsight of later years as a pilot of that particularly well-harmonised aeroplane, the Chipmunk, the flying qualities were fairly peculiar.

Apart from the high drag, which meant that all the flights were short, both of the gliders had fairly simple ailerons; high rolling inertia due to the large wings; and (by powered aircraft standards) relatively ineffective rudders, due to low speed and the absence of propwash.

Turning the aircraft 90 degrees to proceed round the circuit would involve simultaneously applying a fair amount of aileron, accompanied by a very big push on the rudder, and a lowering of the nose to maintain airspeed. What was happening was very significant aileron drag, which had to be overcome by coarse use of the rudder. The nose had to be lowered as the additional aileron and rudder drag could slow the aircraft noticeably in the turn.

Once late downwind, the aircraft would be turned crosswind on to base leg, and then into wind for the finals.

Paradoxically, I remember the final approach as being the highest speed segment of the flight. The airbrakes would be opened, and the nose pushed firmly down to achieve an approach speed which was significantly higher than any other point of the flight (60 kt).

After landing, one would be picked up by a Land Rover towing a Trailer onto which the glider could be mounted for the short trip back to the launch point.

The day of this anecdote was, as it happened, the day of my first solo. Really, it was the ideal day for flying. A clear, sunny summer day, with light winds, and just a scattering of puffy cumulus to indicate that in higher performance gliders, it would be a good day for soaring.

In the event, I was sent off with strict instructions to simply fly round the circuit and land. And to watch out for the climb rate, which would be higher because the glider was lighter. Since this was the Cadet, with its tandem seating, there wouldn't be any noticeable change in drag.

The flight went fine. Probably the scariest part was giving the 'All Out!' command.

Once that was given, everything happened quickly, and pretty much automatically.

Up the climb, speed was good. Don't forget to lower the nose – pull the release, pick up the flying attitude and take stock. All quiet – no instructor shouting from the back; height a little more than usual because of the lighter weight. Turn cross-wind, extending slightly because of the extra height. Down the downwind leg – no real checks.

The normal power ones would be 'Brakes off – no brakes'; Undercarriage down – no undercarriage, just a fixed skid'; 'Mixture rich, Magnetos both, Carb Heat to hot – no engine'; 'Fuel on and sufficient – no fuel'; 'Hatches and Harness – no canopy, just check the straps'. Then, probably the only critical decision, pick the right point to turn base leg, and turn smoothly on to finals. Airbrakes out, nose down to pick up the approach speed, flare, hold, and bump, we're down. After landing, hold the aircraft wings level with the ailerons until the pick-up trailer arrives, and then back to the launch point.

After my first solo, I relaxed on the grass in the sunshine, listening to a transistor radio playing in the background. But then I realised something unusual was happening. Everyone was standing up to watch the Sedbergh going up on the launch.

When I asked what was up, I understood why everyone was watching.

Unbelievably, an attempt was to be made to see if it was possible to loop the Sedbergh, not just once, but three times from a maximum effort 1000 ft launch. And not solo, with a cadet on board as well as the instructor.

The Barge floated sedately off the top of the wire, immediately turned downwind, and then the nose went right down – and up she sailed for the first loop. Over the top, steeply down to pick up speed for the next – up and over again. Now noticeably lower, down with the nose, pick up speed, up and up and stopping, rotating round into a stall turn, vertical for a moment, then a quick aileron turn onto base leg, short finals, and overhead to land.

A few moments of calm, as the glider was picked up on the trailer and brought back.

In the quiet, I noticed the radio playing a new, immediately striking, number. As the shaken cadet emerged from the Land Rover, I heard, for the very first time, the inimitable Procol Harum words 'that her face at first just ghostly, turned a whiter shade of pale'.

Absolutely the perfect end to a perfect day.

A Tandem Tutor (on display in the RAF Museum, Hendon)

Ron Smith

Chapter Two

"We don't charge landing fees for diversions"

Britain has a rich aviation heritage, with aircraft being constructed in all regions. This chapter describes a flight around England to record many of these locations, their companies and products

It was January 1994 and I had just got back to work after the Christmas break. Colin and I were chatting about the holiday, when I asked him if he was familiar with the Dawn to Dusk Trophy. Colin Dodds was a work colleague and also a well-known pilot and author, with many contacts in the de Havilland Moth Club and the Historic Aircraft Association, where he is the current Deputy Chairman.

"Why do you ask?"

"Well, I've had a good idea for a Dawn to Dusk Competition flight".

"Tell me more – having a good idea is the main problem".

By way of explanation, the Dawn to Dusk Trophy is a flying competition invented at the Tiger Club when the Duke of Edinburgh was a member; indeed, the Duke donated the main trophy for the event. The aim of the competition is to encourage the inventive and adventurous use of aeroplanes by demonstrating what can be achieved in the course of a single day.

The rules are disarmingly simple.

During the hours of daylight on a given day normally between mid-April and mid-August, the entrant(s) set off to fly around a route based upon their chosen theme. They are required to spend at least eight hours of the day in the air and must submit a report of their flight within three weeks of its completion. The report must explain why the chosen theme is worthwhile and present background information, flight logs and evidence of the completion of the flight, including photographs of turning points, receipts for fuel uplift and landing fees, etc.

There are a range of awards, which include: recognition for coming in the first three places, with the overall winner receiving the Duke of Edinburgh Trophy; the best report – Tiger Pooley Sword; best solo entry; best entry by an inexperienced crew; long distance trophy; best all ladies entry, and so on.

The Duke of Edinburgh continues to chair the panel of judges.

We had been visiting my in-laws over Christmas and they had been discussing the competition, of which I had been aware from earlier visits to the Tiger Club by push-bike from school in the 1960s. On the drive back home to Somerset, I suddenly had an idea for an entry – it ought to be possible to fly around Britain over locations where aircraft used to be built, by companies that no longer exist.

The only problem I could see was that my own aircraft had too short a range, and it would be far better if the competition flight could be made in a British-built aircraft.

I outlined this idea to Colin, whose response was "What a brilliant idea, why don't you start some planning, whilst I see what I can do about an aeroplane."

A quick look through my own aviation book collection, augmented by three days research in the Royal Aeronautical Society Library in London, generated a list of companies and locations.

Much to my surprise there were a lot of firms building aircraft during the First World War that I had never heard of, my favourite being The Vulcan Motor & Engineering Co (1906) Ltd of Southport who built some 725 aircraft during the War. I decided to position red, green and blue stickers on an aeronautical chart representing 'major / must have'; 'significant / should have' and 'minor / nice to have'. Having given the chart the appearance of an outbreak of some dreadful disease, I settled down to try to find a route that offered the prospect of good coverage for the task.

We needed to avoid Class A airspace and it was obvious that we were unlikely to have the speed and range to cover Scotland as well as England. There also seemed little prospect of penetrating far into the south west, so my old employer, Westland, was also excluded from the list.

The final route extended from Yorkshire and Lancashire down to the south coast, before returning to the Midlands and East Anglia. Based on an assumed endurance of around three hours at 90kt, it looked as if there was scope for a route covering around 600 nm with perhaps three refuelling stops (or two at a pinch).

By the time summer approached we had the bones of a route, but no aircraft.

Then, Colin had a breakthrough, having put the word out in the de Havilland Moth Club that he was looking to borrow an aircraft for a week or so in the summer. Back came David Wells with the amazing news that, as he was planning to be away for a period, Colin could make use of his 1936 de Havilland Hornet Moth biplane for the week.

More than that, there would be no charge other than our own direct costs in terms of fuel and oil, provided that use of the aircraft was kept below 12 hours flying time.

A quick look at the chart revealed that even with the relatively long range of the Hornet Moth, we would not reasonably be able to complete the entire route in a single day. This was significant, as had there been sufficient range, the route could start and finish at the aircraft's home base Little Gransden.

After further investigation, we decided that the aircraft could be moved on the Saturday to the gliding site at Pocklington, a wartime Halifax station, where the Wolds Gliding Club offered overnight accommodation and promised to make hangar space available for the aircraft.

Logistics were a bit of a problem, as even if the flight were successful, we would end up 125 miles from our take off point, where there would be at least one car to collect. After a bit of thought, we decided to drive (two cars) to Little Gransden, where we would meet Mark Miller, who looked after David's aeroplane. My car would stay at Gransden, and I would drive Colin's car to Pocklington.

We got the aircraft out of the hangar and then there was the usual faffing about with refuelling, maps, oil and aircraft documents.

"Colin, is it OK if I head off now?" – I was conscious of the fact that I was driving and Colin would be flying and probably averaging nearly twice my speed. Colin said OK and tossed me his car keys.

This was a mistake, and it was compounded by a separate mistake that I had made earlier.

As I drove north, it slowly dawned on me that we had not removed Colin's headsets from his car. The upshot was that when I arrived at Pocklington, there was no sign of the aircraft, which I had thought would arrive ahead of me.

Colin had had to borrow headsets from Mark, who needed to return home to get them.

Eventually, Colin arrived and I made a grovelling apology. Colin was a little concerned at the apparently high oil consumption on the flight up from Gransden. We put the aircraft to bed and were then shown a pretty basic bunk room in the gliding clubhouse.

The second problem then hit home.

I had not asked what facilities were provided and had blithely assumed we would be staying in a local bed and breakfast.

As it turned out, the room was just a room with two single beds and no bedding.

I had no sleeping bag and no option but to bed down fully clothed, using my leather jacket to try, rather unsuccessfully, to stay warm.

We studied the weather forecast, which indicated that the weather would be perfect, following the clearance of early fog in the Vale of York. This was a potential issue, as we had to be airborne by 0730 if we were to complete our planned route, including fuelling stops, in the hours of daylight.

True to the forecast, it was foggy at 0600, and the fog cleared to a gin-clear summer's day at about 0930. Monday – the same; Tuesday – the same; Wednesday – the same; Thursday – the same.

At least we had the opportunity for some tourism, including visits to the aircraft museum at Elvington and a look at the interesting machines at The Real Aeroplane Company, Breighton.

We also had a tourist visit to York, where the draw of an excellent aviation bookshop in The Shambles proved hard to resist; there was also a visit to Beverley for lunch.

It looked as if Friday would finally offer acceptable weather and we were airborne by 0730 heading for Holme upon Spalding Moor and Sherburn in Elmet, en route to crossing north of Leeds Bradford to Samlesbury, Blackpool and Warton.

To my surprise, air traffic seemed to accept out unusual routeing without the slightest comment.

Colin would call "Golf Lima Oscar 2000 ft on QNH 1020 from Pocklington to Leicester – Navigation competition" and there would be a simple "Roger" and not the slightest question of why an aircraft that was in a navigation competition was headed from Pocklington to Leicester was flying due west, when the direct track would have been almost due south.

The airfields all came up according to plan and were duly photographed as we started to get into the serious business of a route extending over 600 nm with more than 40 turning points.

I should say that our navigation aids comprised a map, a directional gyro, a P-type spirit compass on the floor between the seats and a single VHF radio.

Above: Airbus Broughton on the planned route

Below: The Boulton Paul airfield at Seighford camouflaged by agriculture

Above: Convair 580 on the greasy tarmac at Coventry Airport
Below: The historic airfield at Filton basking in bright sunshine

It was still early as we approached Liverpool flying at low level down the Mersey estuary to photograph Speke and Hooton Park before heading across to the Airbus factory at Broughton.

As we approached the controlled airspace and asked for permission to transit, the friendly controller said "No problem, not above 1500 ft maintaining VFR. I'm expecting an RAF Hawk coming the other way, but you asked first, call westbound for Neston".

After Broughton, the route took us across Staffordshire over the Boulton Paul test airfield at Seighford, now well-camouflaged by agriculture, continuing from there towards our planned landing at Leicester.

"What do you think of the weather, Colin?" I was looking at a dark grey wall of cloud ahead to the east.

"Doesn't look great, let's listen out on the Leicester frequency to see if they are flying".

This was an astute move, as the next thing we heard was Leicester giving their current weather as 300 foot cloudbase and one mile visibility in rain.

"OK, time for Plan B, Ron. I'd like to get on the ground anyway to check the oil consumption, so let's divert to Coventry".

We shut down on a damp, grey, greasy tarmac apron at Coventry next to a DHL Convair 580. I hopped out with the well-named oily rag and wiped off the oil that was trickling down the inside of the undercarriage legs, before it could get as far as the brakes.

A check on the oil contents showed very modest consumption and we came to the conclusion that if you topped it right up, it simply threw out the first half litre, before settling down to a very acceptable burn rate.

After refuelling, we set off on the next leg of the route, to Shoreham on the south coast. Suffice to say, the flight thereafter was routine, except for greyer weather in the east with thick haze, instead of the clear blue skies in the west.

Shoreham's 1930's airport terminal building

The full route flown, with take-off / landing points in *italics*, was Pocklington, Holme on Spalding Moor, Sherburn in Elmet, Leeds Bradford, Samlesbury, Blackpool, Warton, Southport, Speke, Hooton Park, Broughton, Seighford, *Coventry* (diversion), Staverton, Hucclecote, Moreton Valence, Filton, South Marston, Chilbolton, Eastleigh, Sandown, Bembridge, Portsmouth, Middleton on Sea, *Shoreham* (lunch), Rochester, Wisley, Brooklands, Farnborough, Blackbushe, Woodley, *White Waltham*, Booker, Leavesden, Radlett, Hatfield, Luton, Barton-le-Clay, Cranfield, Peterborough, *Little Gransden*.

On arrival at White Waltham, we went to the West London Aero Club to book in and pay for fuel, oil and the landing fee.

When it came to the latter, the duty manager looked up and said "We don't charge landing fees for diversions", Colin said "But, it wasn't …" only to be cut off by the manager "I'll say it again, we don't charge landing fees for diversions!"

When it came down to it, they liked the aircraft and they liked what we were doing with it.

The pioneering airfield and racing circuit at Brooklands

At about 8 pm, we stiffly dismounted from the Hornet Moth and, after a couple of photographs as the sun set, restored her to her hangar after covering some 625 nm in 8.5 hours flying time on a route with some 40 turning points that ranged over much of the length and breadth of England.

With a sigh, we turned to my car and headed back to Pocklington, arriving quite late and finding the clubhouse locked. After a night in the car, we went our separate ways in the morning.

Later in the year, we went to London for the announcement of results and awards. One thing that, in retrospect, we had got right, related to the submission of the report. We had noted that it had to be submitted within three weeks of the flight. We had also noted that there was nothing to stop you writing the report before you flew, so that's what we did. We also, although we were using 3½ inch floppy disks, managed to embed a series of black and white photos of relevant aircraft in the text.

It's hard to believe how difficult and unusual this was in 1994, compared with today's media and memory-rich world.

We added the colour photos taken en route on separate sheets and presented our report in a binder with an evocative photograph of a Miles Falcon on the cover. We also edited our pre-drafted text to reflect the actual route flown including the Coventry diversion.

At the awards ceremony, we received some good-tempered 'joshing' from John Farley, the famous Hawker Siddeley and British Aerospace Harrier test pilot, who had been on the judging panel and said to Colin "Of course, you guys got marked down because you were the most experienced crew". Colin had 6,000 hours total time (5,000 as pilot in command) and was qualified in multi-jet, multi-piston, twin engine and single engine aircraft and helicopters.

Once the reverse order list reached the last three, we realised that we were going to win something. In fact, we were the overall winners and received the Duke of Edinburgh Trophy; a plaque each to keep; and a certificate signed by Prince Philip in his role as Chairman of the judging panel. I subsequently expanded and wrote up the research conducted for the competition into a manuscript, which was published as the five volume series *British Built Aircraft.*

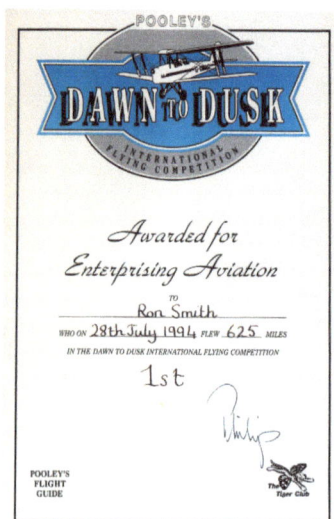

Partially visible engraved text on the trophy:

TIGER ... TROPHY

1965	1966
DON LOVELL	ROBIN VOICE
TURBULENT	TURBULENT

197?	?8
MARILYN WOOD	? HOLMES
ALAN BUTCHER	FOURNIER RF4
CONDOR	

Jim Smith

Chapter Three

"Height - Airframe - Security Engine - Location - Lookout"

A beginner's guide to aerobatics with a real feel for the experience and its challenges.

The Air Training Corps of the 60s was supported by Air Experience Flights located around the country, and in these flights, a succession of generally reservist RAF pilots spent many a happy hour flying Cadets in Chipmunks.

While the express purpose was to provide Cadets an opportunity to fly, the primary aim appeared mainly directed at allowing pilots to enjoy the aerobatic handling qualities of the Chipmunk, with a secondary aim of making Cadets look as green about the gills as possible without them actually being sick.

Individual Cadets reacted differently, but I always enjoyed aerobatics, but often was a little confused because the pilots never told you what they were doing, or what would happen next.

After Cadet flying in the Chipmunk, and later passenger flying in the Wessex Flying Group aircraft whilst at University, I had, like pretty much all those whom have flown the type, fallen in love with it.

A true gentleman's aircraft, stable in the cruise, agile, with powerful and well harmonised controls, although some criticise its lack of rudder authority.

So, after learning to fly on Cessna 150s, and graduating to the Cessna 172, I had joined the Royal Aircraft Establishment Aero Club and converted to flying the Chipmunk, with the firm intention of going on to fly aerobatics myself.

The conversion to the Chipmunk was fairly straightforward, after the initial shock of discovering that on the ground, the aircraft was a real handful until one had learnt to manage the combination of directional instability, poor brakes, and a fully castoring tailwheel. At first encounter, it seemed that full rudder had no effect, and that persistence would then lead to a huge swing, which, after applying full opposite rudder, and a long pause, would lead to a huge swing in the opposite direction. Of course, the moment one opened up the engine for take-off, the resulting series of zig-zags down the (fortunately wide) runway would tell a story to any observer – another new Chippie pilot who hasn't got the hang of it yet.

The Wessex Flying Group Chipmunk G-AOUP approaches to land at Thruxton

The classic lines of the DHC-1 Chipmunk

Eventually, everything became second nature, even including the landings, and it was time to begin learning aerobatics.

A cautionary note to the reader! **DO NOT** attempt any aerobatic manoeuvres without competent instruction. When things go wrong in aerobatics, they can go very badly wrong indeed if the pilot has not been properly trained. At the most benign end of the scale, this can result in an unintended spin; at the most extreme end, to structural failure.
Either way can easily get you **KILLED**.

The first step in learning to fly aerobatics is to become thoroughly familiar with the spin characteristics of the aircraft and to practice the entry and exit from spins in both directions. Because if you mishandle the aircraft in aerobatics, a spin is the most likely outcome. Before any aerobatic manoeuvre, including spins, the first step is to run through the **HASELL** checks. Typically there will be a few items for each letter (and these may differ for different aircraft):

Height – Clear of controlled Airspace; entry height; and lowest height before recovery

Airframe – Brakes off; Gyro compass caged; no loose articles

Security – Canopy closed and locked; straps secure; passenger briefed

Engine – T's and P's in the green; mixture rich; carb heat if required

Location – Identified; away from sensitive areas and airspace restrictions

Lookout – Fly a 360 deg 'clearing turn' looking for other aircraft, not only all around the horizon, but above and below you as well.

For the spin, you select the desired heading, re-check the altitude, and that the carburettor heat has been selected to on and close the throttle.

Hold altitude by gradually bringing the stick back as the speed reduces. In the Chipmunk, as you get to the point of stall, you will feel the stick shake as vortices from the leading edge breaker strips start to impinge on the tail and interact with the elevator.

At that point, the stick is pulled gently but firmly back, at the same time as rudder is applied in the desired direction. The aircraft will seem to pause in the air, and then will roll in the direction in which you have applied the rudder, the nose will drop and the aircraft will enter the spin.

Recovery is straight forward. Opposite rudder is applied and the stick is moved forward until the spin stops (in some cases, and for some aircraft, this may require full forward stick).

At this point the rudder is centralised, and the aircraft can be recovered from the dive.

At the point when the spin stops, it is important to centralise the rudder promptly and bring the stick to a neutral position, otherwise the powerful elevator can easily push you past the vertical, or the rudder can make you slew untidily in the dive.

Once the instructor is happy with the spin recovery, you move on to the aerobatic manoeuvres themselves. For all the manoeuvres, the entry speed has to be right. Too slow, and you are likely to end up in a spin. Too fast, and you might overload the airframe.

For the Chipmunk 120 kts is the normal speed, and this has to be reached in a dive. The routine is the same as learning to fly in general.

First the Instructor demonstrates, then you get talked through the manoeuvre with the instructor following through, and then you demonstrate and practice, with the instructor intervening only if necessary. You will only be cleared to do aerobatics on your own when you have had a check out.

31 3'97

You will need to demonstrate your mastery of the spin, the loop, slow roll and perhaps stall turn, and your ability to recover from "unusual attitudes".

At this point the instructor will say "Close your eyes" and then, after a period of vigorous manoeuvring "Open your eyes, you have control". At this point, you open your eyes and deal with whatever you find.

Two typical situations would be – Upside down, nose below the horizon and dropping, with a definite but not excessive rate of roll; or nose high, speed decaying, high rate of roll and no strong visual cues (it's a cloudless day).

For the first of these the recovery is to check the roll rate and level the wings while pushing (generally quite firmly) to get the nose back up to the horizon.

Once this is done, use the ailerons to roll the aircraft upright, and you're done. For this situation, it is critical not to pull back on the stick.

If you do so, even if the nose is already below the horizon, you can pick up enough speed (and g) as the aircraft accelerates, to either black out, or to break the aeroplane, or both.

For the second, full throttle is applied to help stop the decay in airspeed, stop the roll with the ailerons, and level the wings while pushing the nose back to, or below the horizon to allow speed to pick up.

Again, if you get confused, pulling back on the stick is undesirable. With aft stick, a low airspeed and a rolling aircraft the result is almost certain to be uncomfortable and to end up with the aircraft in a spin.

So, how do you fly a loop? Complete the checks, having first picked a nice straight line on the ground as a reference. I recommend the dual carriageway by the Hen and Chicken pub to the east of Alton myself. Roll out of your clearing turn aligned with the road and hold the nose down while watching the airspeed and RPM.

You are looking for 120 kts, but will need to reduce the throttle to stay within the engine rpm limit.

As 120kts comes up, check you are straight, and pull smoothly back on the stick while opening up to full throttle.

Up she goes – everything goes blue as the horizon drops rapidly out of sight. Don't pull too hard, and as you begin to go over through the top of the loop you will notice how gentle the manoeuvre is – typically the speed will be quite low, and the g will still be positive, but less than 1.0 because of the motion of the aircraft.

Look over your shoulder for the horizon to appear from behind you. Check that the wings are level and, as the ground swings into view above you, look for your reference line, hopefully exactly where it should be.

As the aircraft comes round into the dive, close the throttle (to avoid losing too much height and gaining too much speed), and pull smoothly through.

The g should be no more than about 3 on the initial pull, and perhaps up to 4 on the exit – this is less than a 'good' roller coaster.

A twitch as the aircraft flies through the slipstream at the bottom of the loop – perfect.

Jim Smith

Chapter Four

"Do you want to come up front and have a go?"

Civilians rarely have the opportunity to fly in service aircraft on operational missions. Here, a Royal Australian Air Force maritime patrol aircraft is flown on border protection duties.

Naturally, this is the sort of question for which there is only the one possible answer. "Of course, I'd love to".

At the time, I was sitting in the rear galley area of a RAAF AP-3C Orion, flying relatively low over the water to the North of Darwin.

The aircraft was about 4 ½ hours into its patrol flight, and was about to start the second systematic search pattern of its patrol, which in all would last about 6 hours on this occasion.

Clearly it would not be appropriate to write about the operational aspects of the flight, so I will merely paint a general picture.

What was going on, and how come I was to have the opportunity to fly this aircraft?

Well, the story goes back to a point where four years earlier, I had migrated to Australia with my family to take up a position leading a team providing research and advice to the RAAF on operational tactics, techniques and procedures.

Why had I migrated?

In the UK I had become increasingly discontented and frustrated as changes in the Defence environment pointed towards a diminishing role for the Defence scientific community, with shrinking opportunities for personal growth. This, coupled with some knowledge of the Australian Defence community gained through a role in collaborative projects and research, had prompted me to investigate whether a position in Australia would offer a career path with greater scope for advancement.

So after a brief pause for thought, I found myself picking up a new career within the Australian Defence Organisation. This eventually led to me having an opportunity to observe how the maritime patrol function was being delivered by the RAAF, including the opportunity to observe an Orion crew in action on one of those patrols, with this particular flight operating out of Darwin.

The day had started early, with the crew and scientist observers rendezvousing at 06:00 for a brief, while the air and ground crew ensured that the aircraft systems were on-line and that the day's mission could be delivered. Then it was out to the aircraft, climb aboard and wait for a lengthy period while the crew completed their mission system checks.

And finally, off on patrol. The take-off was an impressive performance, rarely experienced these days.

Large and propeller-driven aircraft have all but disappeared from the main-stream of modern aviation. Such aircraft tend to have a much higher initial acceleration compared to that experienced, for example, on equivalent sized turbo-fan powered civil transport aircraft. And a more impressive and quite different noise, accompanied by vortices streaming off the propeller tips in the warm and humid air of the Northern Territory.

Once airborne and cleaned up, the aircraft settled into a short cruise as we hummed our way over to the first patrol area.

Early morning walk out to the P-3 Orion at RAAF Darwin

There, the crew went about their business while the four scientists aboard observed how they used the systems and interacted together as a crew. Essentially, this involved cooperative use of the various sensors and systems on board to detect and identify a variety of maritime targets, and some specific locations of interest.

After some time of this, the aircraft completed its first assigned patrol area and began a transit to the second area of interest, and I moved back to the galley area to have a cup of tea while watching the tropic sea pass by. At which point, I received my invitation to "have a go".

I made my way forward to the cockpit to find that the left seat had been vacated for me, moving carefully between the seats, I strapped in and donned the headset.

A quick glance around confirmed the situation. We were patrolling at 3000 ft, cruising on three engines at 300 kt.

The port outer engine was shut down and feathered, which appeared to be routine, and had been the situation for most of the flight. The aircraft was being manually flown by the co-pilot, and the weather was largely clear and sunny, but with scattered cumulus between about 1000 and 3000 ft.

Apart from the normal flight instruments, the panel also had an excellent tactical display, on which the various turning points for the second patrol area were displayed, together with the aircraft position and any targets identified by the aircraft radar.

Once I had settled in, the co-pilot said "OK mate – you have control", and there I was, flying the largest, heaviest and fastest aircraft I have ever experienced.

The Orion cockpit offered an excellent view, and also an interesting blend of current and older technologies.

The displays and systems were right up to date, but the overall environment still carried a splendidly retro feel deriving from retained design features going back to the Electra airliner of the fifties, from which the Orion had been developed.

Because of the scattered cumulus, I was looking ahead, using the tactical display and course to steer indicator on the horizontal situation indicator (HSI) to thread my way through the clouds without excessive manoeuvring, which would disturb the sensor operators and without flying through the clouds, not having an instrument rating.

This provided an opportunity to get a feel for the aircraft, so that as I approached the first turning point, I was comfortably able to roll the aircraft to the right and make a 90 degree heading change.

This was fun.

The Orion was relatively easy to fly, and really quite responsive on the controls.

In many ways, like a big Cherokee, but more steady in flight because of the higher inertia.

Oddly enough it shared the other attribute of the Cherokee, being slightly difficult to trim out in pitch – either that, or the crew were walking up and down the aircraft to see how I got on (it has apparently been done).

As I relaxed into flying the aircraft, it was apparent that the crew were in no hurry to move me out, so I continued rounding turning points, and was well through the patrol area when the TACCO (Tactical Commander) came on the intercom and said "OK pilot, put radar target 5 on the nose and descend to 1000 ft".

A quick glance at the display showed the target 30 degrees off to the left.

Roll the aircraft to the left, put the nose down slightly to lose 2000 ft.

OK, the Navigator has put the course to steer into the HSI – continue the turn, and the descent, and then smoothly level out, and there we are, on track and at 1000 ft, below the cloud-base so the imagery operators can identify the target.

I felt very comfortable flying the aircraft, but still cannot get over the experience of tactically manoeuvring this relatively large aircraft to do the required task.

Flying over the ocean at 1000 ft and 300 kts on 3-engines – what a thrill, at least for a relatively low hours private pilot like myself.

All routine for the crew of course, and eventually, after about 45 minutes, the co-pilot said "I know your having loads of fun, Jim, but it's time to give someone else a go".

So I handed the aircraft back, and climbed carefully out of the seat, having flown three quarters of the second patrol area.

My three colleagues then had a few minutes each flying the aircraft.

With no flying experience at all, this resulted in a fair amount of motion, and the complaints from the sensor operators essentially determined how long each of them flew the aircraft.

Once this was complete, the aircraft was nearing Darwin.

The port outer propeller was un-feathered and the engine re-started and everyone returned to their take-off and landing stations and strapped in before we returned to land, after another unforgettable flying experience.

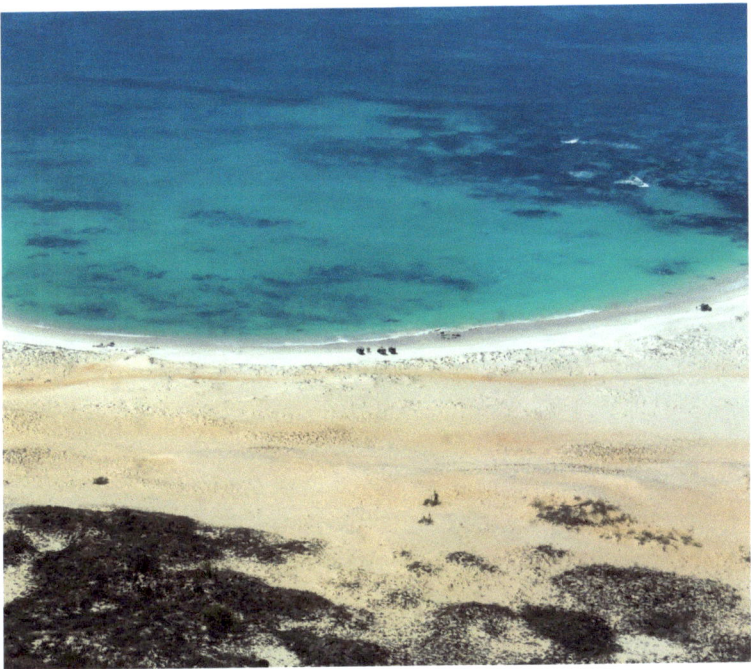

Ron Smith

Chapter Five

"Golf Alpha Yankee Alpha India, are you now happy about your position?"

Flights do not always go to plan; this is a tale of a flight from England to Germany in one of the smallest of aircraft, a Volkswagen-powered motor glider. The adventure includes poor weather, getting lost, engine problems and a landing at a front line fighter base.

It was summer of 1971 and I was on the way to Dahlemer Binz for our second visit to work for Sportavia Putzer, this time through the ten week summer University holiday.

We were both flying from Biggin Hill, me leading the way as passenger in an RF5 motor glider; Jim following the next day in the Sportair Jodel D140.

At this time, neither of us were pilots, although we had done a certain amount of passenger flying and we had both flown solo in basic gliders.

The RF5 sits two in tandem under a long canopy and is powered by a 68 hp Limbach SL1700E engine (basically the engine from a VW Camper Van).

It has a long high aspect ratio wing, which can be folded at part span to reduce the hangarage space required.

The aircraft, like its predecessors, has a retractable undercarriage with a single mainwheel, outrigger wheels beneath the wings being used to prevent the wing tips contacting the ground when taxiing.

When I arrived at Biggin, there was a certain amount of disorder evident. My pilot was in a huddle with Brian and Neil (directors of Sportair), as the aircraft we were due to fly in was busy doing training circuits and showed no sign whatever of wanting to stop. For the purpose of this tale, I do not need to name my pilot, as we ended up having a less-than-routine journey.

Once the aircraft, which was registered G-AYAI, had landed and returned to the club, there was then a bit of a pantomime of loading bags, refuelling and checking the oil level in the engine. This latter was quite tricky. The engine had originally (in its VW application) been installed horizontally in the vehicle's engine bay and had a dipstick to suit. The aircraft had a tailwheel, however, resulting in a nose-up tilt to the engine. Unfortunately, the dipstick was at the front of the engine and all the oil ran to the rear when the aircraft was on the ground.

This rendered the dipstick next to useless as, the 'Full' mark, from its original vehicle application, did not come into play at all. Instead, there was deemed to be sufficient oil in the engine if there was the merest trace of oil on the very bottom of the dipstick.

The aircraft had been flying; the oil was clean and hot; and it was very difficult to withdraw the heat-soaked dipstick without touching it on the crankcase as it was withdrawn. Various attempts were made to check the oil level and I was even asked what I made of it. It was all a bit inconclusive but, being already delayed, it was decided that there was sufficient oil present. The hurry to get on our way militated against what would probably have been the right solution – finding a trestle and using it to raise the tail and check the oil contents in the flight attitude.

We set off, about an hour late in warm sunshine, following the railway line towards Ashford and set course from there for Cap Gris Nez and France.

The elegant lines of Sportavia RF5 G-AYAI

I was completely unused to cross-country flying at the time and was probably less concerned by subsequent events than I would be today.

Half way across the channel, the sea horizon disappeared and we entered cloud.

My pilot cut the throttle and popped the airbrakes and we descended rapidly, breaking cloud over the sea at about 700 feet in considerably reduced visibility.

We crossed the French coast still at about the same altitude and became more or less instantly lost. At 500 feet or so, the ground was visible in a relatively small circle of acceptable visibility, but one could not map-read effectively at that height.

My pilot called Calais for a VFR clearance; they immediately responded "Golf Alpha Yankee Alpha India it is not Visual Meteorological Conditions, you must land here immediately" and then gave a heading to fly.

When we had landed, the controller said that the surface visibility was 1,600 metres (one mile and roughly one third of that required) and of course, as we had found out, the visibility reduced considerably as one flew higher.

Calais – "It is not Visual Meteorologica

So there we were stuck at Calais. After refuelling, clearing customs and cancelling our Flight Plan, the next challenge was to find accommodation for the night. We asked at the airport and received a Gallic shrug. We hired a taxi and asked the driver to take us to a hotel or guest house, only to be told that, for some reason, there were no rooms to be had.

Beggars cannot be choosers and we ended up sharing a double bed in a house that might even have belonged to one of the taxi driver's relatives. Although there was a degree of trepidation with the arrangements, we spent a safe and secure night and were back at the airport early the next morning. We prepared the aircraft and went through the same ritual of ineffectually assessing the amount of oil available.

An additional puzzle was that the windsock was showing an almost flat calm at the surface, whereas the weather brief had suggested a stiff 20 kt form the north.

My pilot decided to split the difference and plan for a 10 kt northerly breeze.

After take-off, we levelled out and I was invited to fly the aircraft. I was in the rear seat and trying to maintain heading using a small ball compass mounted on the instrument panel coaming in the front cockpit. This was tricky, but manageable. After a while flying across that hazy and somewhat featureless area of northern France, we passed just to the north of a town that had a grass airfield on the northern side and an airfield with a hard runway to the south.

This was probably Kortrijk (Coutrtrai) in Belgium (slightly north of track). We, however, concluded that it was Lille about 15 miles to the south, which had the same general layout. In fact, the true track lay between these two, but we were conditioned by the weather forecast to assume that if there was a course error, we would find ourselves south of track.

Thinking that we were at Lille, we changed heading about 10 degrees north and I continued to fly from the back seat.

After a few minutes, I found that I could maintain heading by aiming for some large buildings that were just becoming visible in the distance. My pilot, meanwhile, was studying the chart with some intent. After a few seconds, his head came up and he said "We should be just about at Silly Beacon".

This immediately caught my attention as, when we had flown from Biggin to Dahlemer Binz non-stop in the Jodel in the spring, we had flown directly overhead this VOR, which was near the town of Ath south west of Brussels; in fact, we had seen it sitting in the middle of open farmland. I pointed out to the pilot that I was aiming at large buildings ahead, which didn't look right.

He said "Damn! Brussels Hotel de Ville" and turned about 30 degrees to the right.

At this point, and fearing that we might have infringed controlled airspace, he decided that it was time for some help. Now, the RF5 was not really equipped as a touring aircraft and had a very basic glider-type crystal-controlled radio, with only 11 or 12 channels. As a result, there was little option but to call on the emergency frequency of 121.5 MHz.

There was an immediate response from Beauvechain, who, on learning of our approximate position said "Golf Alpha Yankee Alpha India we are active with fast jet traffic in that area. Please climb to 2500 metres".

Now 2500 metres is more than 8,000 feet, which is a big ask for a Volkswagen-powered motor glider. Anyway, we duly began a lengthy climb, whilst Beauvechain gave us some headings to fly.

Eventually, we levelled out and the Beauvechain controller called "Golf Alpha Yankee Alpha India, are you now happy about your position?"

We said that we were.

Almost as we replied, the oil pressure suddenly dropped to near zero and we informed Beauvechain "We are returning to your position for a precautionary landing".

The pilot asked me to look at his flight guide and see what

the runway length was. I replied that there were two runways 04/22 left and right, each more than 8000 ft long. As we headed back, the airfield asked for our type and asked us to join for 04 left. Could we accept a three mile final?

The pilot replied "Negative, joining base leg for one mile finals 04 left", explaining to me that he didn't want a longer approach in case the engine stopped.

As we approached the airfield from the south it became apparent that 04 right was active with SIAI Marchetti SF260 training aircraft that proceeded to fly around us as we crossed their approach path.

Turning finals, with the undercarriage down, the runway controller asked us to check that we had 'three greens', confused no doubt by the single main wheel of the RF5. As we crossed the airfield boundary, we saw a pair of F-104 Starfighters waiting for us to land.

We turned left off the runway at the first opportunity and watched with some awe as the Starfighters blasted off as soon as we were clear.

The waiting Starfighters blasts off from Beauvechain

Quite a lot happened after that. A fire tender arrived, closely followed by a truck full of armed troops.

Air traffic asked what our requirements were, to which the pilot replied that we needed "aircraft engine lubricating oil".

Beauvechain replied that they had a range of US / NATO standard lubricants available... This seemed to complicate matters unnecessarily, so we replied "What we really need is Volkswagen engine oil; 20/50Q would be fine".

There was a slightly glum noise at the other end followed by "We'll have to ask Motor Transport". Whilst this was going on, a police car arrived.

They wanted to see all personal and aircraft paperwork and proceeded to stamp pretty much all of it. I had the stamp of Le Commandant de la Brigade de Gendarmerie de Beauvechain in my passport for quite a few years. The man from Motor Transport duly turned up with a 2 litre can of oil and an 'I've been had' expression on his face.

We welcomed him enthusiastically and having topped up the engine, completed a successful, leak-free, ground run and filed a new flight plan, we were free to continue our journey.

From Beauvechain, we had a smooth and untroubled flight past Liege and over Spa, before landing at Dahlemer Binz.

On arrival, we found that we were no longer the advance party, as the Jodel had arrived about an hour earlier. We also found that none of the Flight Plan cancellations or updates had reached our destination and, as we were now 25 hours late, they were wondering whether something needed to be done about it.

Safely on the ground at Dahlemer Binz

Ron Smith

Chapter Six
"Three to a Room"

An American road trip from Tucson to Las Vegas with an aeronautical backdrop

It is February 1981 and I am, somewhat to my surprise, Head of Future Projects at Westland Helicopters Ltd. The company has developed the WG30 for the civil market, making use of the Lynx dynamic system attached to a new high-capacity fuselage.

It would be fair to say that the new product is not taking the market by storm and I had been asked to review options that would make it more successful. The nub of the problem is, perhaps, best summed up by the results of a light-hearted naming competition in the Technical Office.

The winner, hands down, was Westland Wardrobe. The three strands of logic behind this were as follows, its proponent explained: Westland helicopters (and aircraft) should begin with a 'W', as in Widgeon, Whirlwind and Wessex. Finally, and specific to the WG30, it should be called Wardrobe because it looked like one, and the killer argument was that, like a wardrobe, when it was full, you couldn't move it very far. The aircraft offered payload, but inadequate range.

In this environment, it was decided that three of us myself, Graham and David, would attend the Helicopter Association International Convention in Las Vegas, with an opportunity to meet potential customers (David and Graham were in the marketing department) and look at competitor aircraft.

Once the trip was mooted, the three of us got together and hatched out a plot. This was, in essence, that we should travel to the US a week earlier than required taking this as holiday. David had a friend in Dallas, whom he knew when they were studying at Cranfield University. She was married and he had a long-standing invitation to go and stay with the family. A quick telephone call established that she had no objection to a couple of other guests turning up.

Graham and I were both interested in aviation and, given that it was unfair to descend mob-handed on the Dallas couple for an entire week, we suggested that after a long weekend in Dallas, we should head off to Tucson before flying on from there to Las Vegas. We would fund this by cashing in our tickets to Vegas when we reached Dallas.

We picked Tucson because it was the home of the MASDC (pronounced MASDIC), which was the Military Aircraft Storage and Disposal Center, now known as AMARC, the Aerospace Maintenance and Reutilization Center, both being popularly known as The Boneyard.

Dallas was fun; we were given a quick tour of favourite places and went to the cinema (seeing Indiana Jones & the Temple of Doom, if my memory serves me well). After that, we headed out to South Fork Ranch (of Dallas TV fame) and then did some pretend real estate shopping.

This was extraordinary – I had no idea that American real estate taste could be so bad! We saw faux French chateaux and plastic Tudor England. Every feature that the agent waxed lyrical about made us cringe more – and these were properties with prices upward of $1.2m! I think that we finally packed it in when Dave described one particular agent's priceless gem as "like the Wopalino Embassy".

Westland's WG30 for the civil market

What we did realise when we got to Dallas was that, because air fares to Las Vegas are highly competitive, the cash return for ours (after flying on to Tucson) left no hope of air travel from Tucson to Vegas.

We decided that that was a problem for another day, however.

On Tuesday evening, we arrived in Tucson, circling to land over a vast sea of apparently abandoned aircraft.

Several compounds near the airport also featured a number of larger piston engine aircraft, such as Constellations and Stratocruisers. In the terminal, we found an accommodation list with contact details.

A couple of phone calls and a taxi ride saw us arriving at a down-market hotel where we further conserved our limited resources by sharing three-to-a-room.

The priority on the Wednesday was to get wheels.

MASDC a veritable sea of apparently abandoned aircraft

The hotel gave us directions to the nearest hire car company, which had a branch about a mile away.

We decided to walk, rather than take a taxi.

This was such an un-American activity, that we were immediately marked out as strangers in town.

It was actually a shock to find that there was no pavement or sidewalk provided in the residential area that we were crossing.

Even more of a surprise was to be stopped and quizzed by the local police, who wanted to know what we were doing and didn't seem to feel that 'walking' was a wholly adequate answer.

This was pretty speedily resolved, but I suspect that a careful eye was kept on us, until we reached the car hire firm.

We headed for the entrance to MASDC, where we knew that there were guided tours every Wednesday … wrong!

A regatta of B-52 tail fins

In these internet-enabled days, it may seem surprising that we had no idea that we had arrived on February 22nd, George Washington's birthday and a public holiday, with the result that the facility was closed.

At least the gate security personnel were friendly; they told us that we should visit the Pima County Air Museum, which was largely made up of interesting aircraft drawn from the redundant MASDC fleet.

"Guys, we're really sorry that we can't help. After you visit the museum, just take a drive round the perimeter. You'll get a pretty good view and nobody will pay any attention, we get people doing that all the time.

Close to, the analogy of a sea of aircraft seemed even more appropriate, as the tall tail fins of early model B-52 bombers gave the immediate impression of a fleet of large racing yachts, jockeying for starting positions at Cowes regatta.

The Pima County Museum was nothing short of brilliant.
It was packed with early jets and later fighters, with a
sprinkling of the rare and unusual thrown in.

Boeing B-47 Stratojet at the Pima Air Museum

Just to give some examples, the types included Lockheed Starfire; Grumman Panther, Cougar and Tiger; Convair / General Dynamics F-102, F-106 and Hustler; North American F-107 and Vigilante; Lockheed Constellation and Warning Star; Douglas B-18 and B-23; Curtis Commando; Northrop Raider; Kaman Huskie – and on and on in that vein.

Above: Surviving Boeing 307 Stratoliner; it was later restored to flying condition by the Boeing Company

Top Left: Douglas B-23 Dragon – just one of the rare exhibits at Pima Air Museum
Middle Left: Grumman F-11F Tiger one of the many naval exhibits
Bottom Left: Boeing B-52 adapted to carry and drop the North American X-15 research aircraft

Below: This Kaman HOK-1 is one of several unusual helicopters on display

The McCulloch MC-4A. Two examples were evaluated by the US Navy as the XHUM-1

Above: Another naval helicopter, the Vertol HUP-1 Retriever. 339 examples of this successful type were built

Below: The Lockheed WV-2 Warning Star was an Airborne Early Warning and intelligence gathering derivative of the Lockheed Constellation

Above: The portly Douglas B-18B Bolo, a DC-2 derivative adapted as a bomber and also used for anti-submarine patrols

Below: A less-than pristine Douglas Invader at Tucson Airport Storage and Restoration Facility

Tucson Airport Storage and Restoration Facility

A Douglas C-133 Cargomaster – one of the most imposing turboprop aircraft. 50 were built and several survive

Above: A Boeing Stratocruiser in Aero Spacelines colours. This aircraft was broken up in 1982

Below: This Curtiss C-46 Commando also awaits its turn for restoration

Above: Another rare survivor, this Northrop YC-125A Raider sits in the desert sun awaiting restoration

Below: Douglas C-124 Globemaster II heavy military transport, one of 448 built

Above: An engineless DC-7, previously operated by American Airlines

Below: An immaculate Convair 440 in the Arizona sun

Above: Another rare bird, DHC4 Caribou N518N. This aircraft was sold to Ecuador and was scrapped after an accident

Below: Columbia XJL-1 at Tucson Airport, subsequently displayed at the Pima Air Museum

Grumman E-1 Tracer Carrier Airborne Early
Warning aircraft sit beached at MASDC

MASDC and surrounding scrapyards

Above: LTV F-8 Crusaders in one of the scrapyards that surround MASDC

Below: A forlorn group of US Marine Corps CH-37 Mojave await the scrapman's axe at one of the local yards

As an added bonus, the museum was surrounded by scrapy-ards, which at the time were full of Grumman Trackers and Traders; LTV F-8 Crusaders; Sikorsky H-34s; and other types being 'reduced to produce'.

In addition to its vast fleet of B-52s, the main storage area featured Martin B-57 Canberras and its long-winged RB-57 derivative.

We also saw Douglas C-117s, Lockheed Constellations; Fairchild Providers; Boeing KC-97s and numerous other types.

All in all, we had an excellent day, despite our initial dis-appointment. We retired to another salubrious shared room on the north side of Tucson, for the princely sum of $22 for three.

The next day we set off on the trip to Las Vegas via Flagstaff, driving through the desert in bright, warm sunshine.

This colourful Grumman Tracker was one of many to be seen awaiting disposal or scrapping at facilities adjoining MASDC

Ron Smith

Chapter Seven

"Do you want to sit in the left hand seat?"

Sometimes one can hitch a ride in another pilot's aircraft; even better, this can lead to lasting friendships and the opportunity to fly over spectacular landscapes in old and unusual types.

We had all agreed that driving to Flagstaff via the interstate system would be just too dull, so we opted for a cross country route, travelling on Route 77 via Mammoth (where we stopped for a burger – a Mammoth Burger, as we styled it) and Globe, from where we headed off on the Apache Trail towards the Theodore Roosevelt Lake. We travelled some of this route on unmetalled roads, before reaching Payson and winding our way from there through Pine, Strawberry up to the Mogollon Rim and thence via Happy Jack and the Mormon Lake to Flagstaff.

This was a brilliant trip and gave us a real view of back-country Arizona.

From the Saguaro (organ pipe) cactus of the Sonora Desert area around Tucson, the route climbed more or less continuously as we headed north. Tucson's elevation is 2,600 ft, whereas Flagstaff is at some 7,000 ft, with the San Francisco Peaks nearby rising above 12,600 ft.

Consequently, by the time we arrived in Flagstaff after a full day driving, it was already dark and the temperature was well below freezing, with snow on the ground.

It was sobering to realise that we were still in the same State, where the morning trip had started at 70°F, in bright sunshine.

At Flagstaff, we achieved our lowest cost accommodation of the trip at $20 for three, complete with coin-operated vibrating bed. Next morning, we were up early and it was my turn to drive. An interesting experience, as it was the first time that I had driven an automatic, it was also my first time in a left-hand drive car and the roads were slippery. We drove north towards the Grand Canyon, past the San Francisco Peaks. The road levelled off and I was presented with a classic scene of the American west. The road ran straight ahead to the horizon, which was itself arrow straight and uninterrupted by any man-made feature – no buildings, no power lines, not even any telegraph poles. Talk about 'big skies'!

Once we approached the Grand Canyon South Rim, we found that we could charter a helicopter or fixed wing aircraft for a flight in the Grand Canyon. We opted for a Bell 206 Jet Ranger and by pooling our resources were able to have an unforgettable flight.

Most memorable was skimming low over the trees of the rim at about 100 kts and then suddenly flying out into the canyon over a sheer drop of perhaps 2,000 ft.

After around 40 minutes, we returned to the airport and drove up to stand on the rim itself. One phenomenon that was apparent was the psychological reduction of the scale of the grandeur to a level that the brain could cope with. We looked across at a prominent feature and discussed how far away it was; the consensus was around two miles. Reference to a map showed, however, that it was at least eight miles distant. It is literally hard to comprehend the true scale of the Grand Canyon.

a Bell 206 Jet Ranger

We headed down to the iconic Route 66, taking "the highway that is best" from Flagstaff to Kingman, from where we could strike out north-east toward the Hoover Dam, Boulder City and Las Vegas.

At Kingman, we (fairly typically) headed for the airport, which was littered with various redundant and decommissioned airliners in the process of being scrapped.

The road from the airport back to Kingman was something of 'Trailertown, USA', and we saw there what was definitely the cheapest accommodation on offer – 'Rooms: $10 for one; $12 for two and $14 for three".

The town itself was 'Traintown, USA' with the mournful blues wail of Amtrak providing the soundtrack.

An enormous Santa Fe Railroad steam locomotive is preserved at Kingman as a monument to the town's links with the tracks. As we left Kingman, the skies were darkening to a deep shade of purple that presaged a desert storm.

We drove past the sign-posted ghost towns to the dramatic accompaniment of lightning to our left and tumbleweed bowling across the road. We stopped to look at the Hoover Dam – undeniable impressive, particularly given the 725 ft drop from top to bottom of the dam structure.

As evening approached, we crested some high ground to find the glittering constellation of Las Vegas set out in front of us in the desert.

Like all such conventions, the HAI gathering was a bit of an ordeal, with too much standing around and stands manned by sales and marketing personnel, who seemed to be there mainly to prevent one having a meaningful conversation with anyone who mattered. The show had organised a display of the latest helicopter models on the ramp at McCarran International airport with a regular bus service from the Convention Center. McCarran, like a number of other fields in the western desert sates, seemed to be a temporary home for a number of obsolescent airliners looking for new owners, or simply in temporary storage.

Above: A Korean Airlines Boeing 707 being scrapped at Kingman

Below: One of a number of DC-8s being 'reduced to produce' under the threatening Kingman skies

Above: Prototype Boeing 747 N7470 stored at Las Vegas

Below: The splendid Scenic Airlines 'Tin Goose'

To our surprise, this included the original Boeing 747 prototype N7470 stored awaiting its next role as an engine test bed for Boeing. Pleasingly, the new helicopter display took place just outside Scenic Airlines facility and gave access to the aircraft parking ramp.

Scenic have, for many years, carried out aviation tours of the Grand Canyon, mainly using de Havilland Canada Twin Otters modified with large windows to provide the passengers with superlative views and maximum photographic opportunities. At this time, however, they were still operating 1929 Ford 5-AT Trimotor N414H, with their hangar being emblazoned with "Scenic – Home of the Tin Goose".

Back at the show, by Saturday, Graham and I were completely worn out with helicopters and decided that we deserved the afternoon off to see if there were any interesting aircraft at North Las Vegas airport, a general aviation field located, not surprisingly, on the north side of the city.

Globe Swift and Temco Swift. Jess Meyers' aircraft in the foreground prior to conversion to Buick V8 power

Once there, we found plenty of interest, including a pair of Globe Swifts parked next to each other, with a gentleman working on one of them. After saying hello and introducing ourselves, we discovered that Jess lived locally and that his wife Marion worked for the Convention Center and had been liaising with the HAI for the helicopter convention.

"Is this a Globe Swift, or a Temco Swift?" I asked.

"Oh, this one's a Globe, the yellow one is a Temco", Jess replied.

We asked if we could come back and photograph the two aircraft once he had replaced the engine cowlings. After doing so, Jess asked if we were pilots and Graham said that we were both interested in all forms of aviation, but that I had a pilot's licence. I said that I had learned to fly in 1978 and currently had less than 100 hours total time and was current on the Tiger Moth and Cessna 172.

"Have you seen Las Vegas from the air?" No.

"Well, there's a Cessna behind us, why don't we go flying?"

We said we'd be delighted, if that was really alright with him. "Which one of you wants to sit in the front?" I was extremely pleased when Graham said that, as I had the pilot's licence, I should have the honour. I headed for the starboard (passenger) door and then Jess said "Do you want to sit in the left hand seat?"

I did a quick double-take; here was someone whom I had just met, who only had my word for it that I flew, asking if I wanted to sit in the pilot's seat of his aircraft. "Are you sure that's OK" I asked, mindful of the fact that I also didn't have a US Airman's Certificate.

"Oh, you'll be fine. I'm instructor-rated and if I don't like the way you're flying, I'll just take over". We strapped in to the Cessna 175 that Jess explained belonged to his father. He started the engine, made some radio calls, taxied and lined up with the active runway.

He turned to me "It's all yours".

Above: The Cessna 175 flown by the author from North Las Vegas

Below: Bad territory for a forced landing in the vicinity of Boulder City

I opened the throttle, kept straight and lifted off, noting the unusually high rpm due to the geared engine. At 300 feet, I turned to ask Jess what rpm I should throttle back to, only to find that he had already turned round and was talking to Graham in the back.

We flew out staying clear of McCarran and then past Boulder City to the Hoover Dam. The landscape did not look appealing, should there be an engine failure. When I mentioned this to Jess, he laughed and said cheerfully "With a bit of care, you can survive the forced landing – it's the rattlesnakes that will get you!"

The air was incredibly smooth, which flattered my flying considerably. Visibility was excellent, although a blue haze in the distance clearly showed which way California lay.

We arrived at the Dam with perfect timing, as the sun was shining directly down the exit gorge, lighting the dam directly, rather than it being hidden in the shadow.

We flew from there across the desert, staying just below the airspace of Nellis Air Base, although looking across to starboard, we could just make out a multitude of aircraft ranged out on their acres of concrete apron, including at least ten B-52s and a number of KC-135s.

Following Jess's directions, I headed back to North Las Vegas which, as Jess pointed out, was relatively easy to find because of the nearby drive-in movie screens.

As we approached the field, he dealt with the radio calls and guided me into the pattern. He then said "Well, you're flying so well, I don't see why I should spoil it by doing the landing!" I was a bit late getting the flap down and consequently landed a little long, but otherwise safely enough. Jess went on to modify his Swift to take Buick V-8 power, with a belt reduction unit of his own design. With the Buick, the aircraft looked and sounded like a mini Hurricane, with an under-fuselage radiator and eight crackling stub exhausts. That chance meeting was the start of a thirty-year friendship between Hilary and I and Jess and Marion.

Jess' 1950 V-tail Beech Bonanza

We have stayed with each other as guests and flown in each other's aircraft.

I did one of my best landings ever in Jess's 1950 ''B-model' Bonanza – complete with its throw-across flight controls. (The passenger sits with an empty space in front of him and when it's time to take control, the pilot presses a button and swings the whole control wheel across the cockpit to literally hand over the controls. This bringing new meaning to the phrase "You have control".)

I followed up the Bonanza flight with three horrible landings in a Buick-engined Vans RV-6A, where I was flaring too high, possibly as a result of having just got out of the Bonanza. Thanks to Jess's generosity and his ability to persuade others to let me fly in their aircraft, I flew in both of the Swifts, the Bonanza, Buick RV-6A, Ryan Navion and, scariest of all, an RLU Breezy, all from North Las Vegas.

That chance meeting was the start of a thirty-year friendship between Hilary and I and Jess and Marion. We have stayed with each other as guests and flown in each other's aircraft.

The Breezy is breezy by name and breezy by nature.

There is no external fuselage structure, just a tubular steel spine instead of a fuselage. Sat on the bench seat, with only a lapstrap, I was conscious of the fact that the only solid surface in the cockpit was the sheet on which I was resting my feet, and that was made of transparent perspex. It all felt very insecure. The particular example that I flew had been built up using an Aeronca wing, tail feathers and engine.

I noticed that it had large endplates on the wing tips and next to no dihedral. I wonder if that was responsible for the strange landing characteristics. As one entered ground effect in the flare, it suddenly wobbled left and right at quite a high frequency, like a weight shift microlight in turbulence.

Apart from that, and the feeling of insecurity engendered by the lack of a shoulder harness and the extreme field of view, it was quite alright, really.

The RLU Breezy provided a unique flying experience

Above: The two Swifts at North Las Vegas. The nearer aircraft has been converted to Buick V8 power

Below: Crackling exhausts and an underbelly radiator transform the Swift into a mini-Hawker Hurricane

Above: The author and his instructor after a flight in the Breezy

Below: Smooth landings in the Buick-engined RV6A proved to be a challenge

Jim Smith

Chapter Eight

"Sorry, Jim, your ride is in the Mitchell, not one of the Mustangs"

Occasionally, the opportunity arises for an extraordinary aviation experience. In this case, Jim takes a flight around southern California in a mixed group of Second World War Mustangs and Mitchells.

It was 1991, and the first Gulf War has recently ended. There was a general feeling of relief in the air, and also a feeling that the alliance between the USA and the UK had been tested and proven to be strong.

The air war in Iraq had tested the capabilities of the alliance air forces in combat, and against sophisticated ground defences. The new Stealth Fighters had shown what they could do in operations, and the RAF had made significant contributions, with their key strike aircraft, the Tornado GR1 having capabilities for low-level airfield attack, and for tactical reconnaissance not available to the US at the time.

In California, the organisers of the Compton Air Show felt that it would be right to honour the contribution made by the RAF in the conflict.

To deliver this, they conceived the notion of inviting a senior RAF Commander, and one of the Tornado pilots who had been shot down in action, to come to the Air Show.

The invitation was to be made more technically relevant by a series of briefings and visits, and from this stemmed perhaps the most interesting and satisfying few days of my period working in the British Embassy in Washington.

My role was to develop and foster relationships and cooperation between the US and UK aerospace community, primarily working with NASA and the USAF on international collaborative projects.

My report on the F-117 had shown the Air Force Staff that there was value in having a knowledgeable specialist attend technical visits, and I was invited to come along to brief the VIP visitors on the technical aspects of the program being established.

The Technical Program

The tour party consisted of our VIP guest, his wife, and his aide-de-camp; the Tornado pilot and his wife; a Group Captain from the RAF staff and myself.

Not everyone attended all the events, and it would not be appropriate to discuss all of the detail.

The proposed program was extraordinary, and even though not everything planned came off, the eventual program was quite astonishing.

In summary, the program spread over 2½ days, and started with a visit to 'The Big Blue Cube', the headquarters of US Space Command, from which the then new constellation of GPS satellites were being managed.

This was followed by an opportunity for me to provide a technical pre-brief in advance of the visit program for the next day, which was to include a program of visits to Palmdale and Edwards Air Force Base, followed by a gala dinner at the Beverly Wilshire Hotel and then on the final day, the Compton Airshow itself.

The visit to Palmdale and Edwards started from the Northrop facility at Hawthorn, from where we flew in a company aircraft to Palmdale.

The first item on the program was a tour of the B-2 production facility.

At this time two B-2 aircraft had flown, and the third was in final check out.

From a technical standpoint, the aircraft is a stand-out of aerodynamic optimisation, with the flying wing configuration allowing long range and large payload, while careful control of geometry, materials and coatings provide very low radar signature.

It was extraordinary to receive a briefing on this aircraft and its capabilities. At one point we were told that 900 new materials or processes had been developed to build the aircraft.

To which, I have to admit that my reaction was – no wonder it's so expensive!

From the Northrop plant, we moved across to visit the Rockwell production line upgrading the F-111 and converting Lockheed C-130 transport aircraft into the AC-130U gunship.

Then, on to the Rockwell flight test facility to see the Rockwell-DASA X-31 high manoeuvrability test aircraft, with its carbon paddles providing a thrust vector capability.

Another personal highlight was to see the two chase planes for this program – probably the last RF-8U Crusaders operating in the world. Not content with this feast of advanced technology, the next step was to move across the street to the Space Shuttle refurbishment facility.

There we viewed Columbia, which had returned from space just nine days previously and was undergoing inspection before being readied for the next mission.

The visit included walking underneath the shuttle, which was on jacks, viewing the streaks and chips in the protective heat tiles, which would be repaired as necessary before the next flight.

There was also an opportunity to walk up to the access door and view the inside of the shuttle, and the thermal blankets that insulate the upper fuselage.

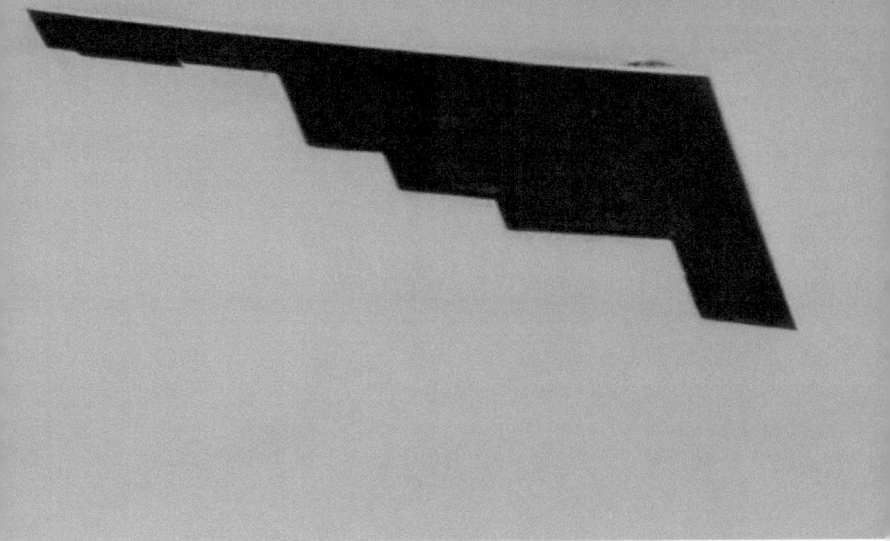

Above and Below: The Northrop B-2 Spirit displaying for the Pentagon and politicians at Andrews Air Force Base 1991

Above: The Space Shuttle Columbia in the refurbishment facility, later to be tragically lost on re-entry.

Below: The upper fuselage and maneouvring engine pod of Columbia, showing the insulating blanket over the fuselage sides.

Lockheed AC-130U on the flight test ramp at Edwards Air Force Base

The party had lunch and then hopped in the Northrop-owned King Air for the short flight up to Edwards.

At Edwards, the program was a little disappointing, as the appropriate clearances had not materialised.

Nevertheless, the opportunity was provided to get up close and personal to the F-15 Eagle; an AC-130 test aircraft and to tour inside and out a Rockwell B-1B Lancer.

The B-1B had only recently been declared operational and had not seen service in the First Gulf War.

It has subsequently become a mainstay of operations, serving with distinction in both the Second Gulf War and the subsequent conflict in Afghanistan.

The Rockwell B-1B at Edwards AFB

Above: Clay Lacy's immaculate racing Mustang sits on the ramp at Compton

Below: A Cavalier Mustang from Chino – was there ever a more handsome aircraft?

The Compton Airshow

The following morning, the four RAF officers and I headed out to the Compton Airshow. The number of aircraft, and their quality and interest was amazing. Everything from a Curtiss Commando to a Harlow PJC-2. And a row of gleaming Mustangs, with Mitchells, an Invader and numerous Harvards. We learned that the plan was for the contribution of the Allies in the Gulf War to be celebrated by flying members of our group in the rear seat of the Mustangs, and that they would directly participate in the Compton Airshow.

At first, it seemed likely that I would fly in one of the Mustangs, but in the event, I drew the short straw and was told "Sorry, Jim, your ride is in a Mitchell, not one of the Mustangs".

I was assigned to fly in 'Heavenly Body', certainly the smartest looking of the four Mitchells to participate in the formation. As things turned out, this was a good outcome for me, because I was able to move about in the Mitchell and use my camera, and the RAF team all found the Mustang cramped and not offering a very good view from the rear seat.

So my next move was to climb aboard 'Heavenly Body', strap in to a seat immediately behind the pilots and make myself comfortable. The Mitchell is a rugged medium bomber from the Second World War and significant numbers have survived, particularly in the USA, where they have seen service in a variety of civil roles, from transport to agriculture.

They have also been used in some numbers as film platforms, for which they offer space, stability and a range of filming positions including the nose, two waist gun positions and a tail gunner station.

The aircraft is powered by two Pratt & Whitney radial engines, which have quite short exhaust stacks and which idle rather unevenly, with a characteristic ragged clatter as occasional misfires occur at low rpm.

Above: The office of 'Heavenly Body' runs through the checklist - Below: 4 Mustangs formate below us

Above: 'Executive Sweet' over California - Below: A rhapsody in blue, the 4th Mitchell in US Navy colours

The aircraft is powered by two Pratt & Whitney radial engines, which have quite short exhaust stacks and which idle rather unevenly, with a characteristic ragged clatter as occasional misfires occur at low rpm. From inside the aircraft, as we taxi out to take off, this sounds exactly as if someone is periodically slapping the side of the aircraft with an open hand. Pleasingly, however, this only happens at low rpm, and everything becomes smooth as we take-off.

'In the Mood' enjoying the southern sunshine

After take-off, the formation assembles, and off we go. The formation is led by the Mitchells, with 'Heavenly Body' being accompanied by 'Executive Sweet'; 'In the Mood'; and an unnamed example in US Navy colours. Behind and generally below the Mitchells, are the four Mustangs, with a Douglas Invader and a Harvard in trail behind the formation, whilst a Learjet weaves over the formation filming the event. Once airborne, I was expecting that we would join up, and maybe fly a few passes over the Airshow crowd before landing.

But it turned out that the plan included not only the Compton airshow, but visits to over-fly other airfields in Southern California. Because of the extended nature of the flight, I was able to move freely about the aircraft, taking air-to-air pictures of other Mitchells, and enjoying the spectacular aircrafts and the passing California scenery. Chino airfield was the home base for some of the Mustangs and once there, the Mitchells made a low pass down the runway at about 250 ft. Only, of course, to be upstaged by the Mustangs, that swept through in formation, passing directly underneath the four Mitchells as they did so.

What a great few days. It was a real privilege to have been part of the technical visit and the Compton Air Show, 1991.

Ron Smith

Chapter Nine

"This is a water landing so the wheels are ...up!"

This story demonstrates both the delights and dangers of the addictive combination of wings and floats.

Flying floatplanes (or seaplanes, as they are known in the UK) has been described as offering all the challenges of flying and sailing at the same time.

What does this mean in practice; what's so different?

First, a health warning: this story is written by a pilot, who has only experienced a single day of seaplane flying.

My Westland colleague David Shepherd held a Seaplane Rating and was tremendously enthusiastic about all forms of water aviation. After gaining considerable experience flying the Tiger Club's seaplane Tiger Moth, David decided to see if he could persuade Norman Jones, who ran the Club, to put G-AVPT, one of their Piper PA-18 Super Cubs, on floats.

In principle, this should be a more practical mount than the Tiger, offering easier operation and better performance, and the prospect of setting up a UK training operation for pilots wanting to gain a Seaplane Rating. In practice, however, this was by no means straightforward.

The type had not been certificated before on floats in the UK; there were also no floats available; and the Tiger Club's water operating base at Scotney Court was unlicensed. (Flying training could only be conducted at a licensed airfield or, as in this case, licensed water).

David was not about to let these minor hindrances stand in the way.

Fortunately, the aeronautical water world is quite a close-knit community and David was able to locate a set of Super Cub floats and struts … in Switzerland.

After agreeing the sale price, this merely required an expedition across Europe towing a trailer to collect them.

Having secured the 'boots', the next tasks were to obtain CAA approval for operation of the Super Cub on floats in the UK and for the licensing of Scotney Water near Dungeness in Kent.

David tackled the former and found out the requirements for the latter, which the Club set about implementing.

Above: The unmodified aircraft at Redhill for familiarisation flying
Below: G-AVPT beached at the edge of the licensed water at Scotney Court

Key to the aircraft certification process was a demonstration that the float struts and their attachments to the fuselage could react all to the required landing loads at acceptable stress levels.

Fortunately, David was an experienced stress engineer, working in a helicopter design and manufacturing organisation, so was able to tackle this task and present the relevant information with confidence.

Thus it was that, after several months of effort, the design had been approved and the water licensed.

David, being well aware of my interest in the more unusual fringes of aviation, invited me to fly with him from Redhill in the Super Cub, at that time not yet fitted with floats.

I think that he was lining me up as a candidate for seaplane training from the outset.

This initial flight at least gave me some familiarity with flying the Super Cub and also the limited view available from the back seat with David up-front.

The aircraft was moved to Scotney Court and fitted with the floats, prior to a two week session of flying training. The initial objective was to allow pilots already holding seaplane ratings to renew them. It also allowed all the procedures for safe operation to be exercised.

Passenger flying was then encouraged to raise the profile of the operation among Club members with a view to persuading more individuals to 'take the plunge'.

Thus it was that, one windy day in September 1985, David drove me across the length of southern England from Somerset to Kent. I asked what I should bring with me, to which the answer was, somewhat ominously, Wellington boots. We arrived at the Scotney Court gravel pit to find a bright sunny day and the wind blowing half a gale.

There were decent size wavelets and clear wind streaks on the water. David seemed not in the least disconcerted by the windiness of the day, declaring it to be an excellent day for seeing the operation in practice.

Like ballooning, seaplane operation is a team activity; there was a safety boat to man and it was very useful to have a knowledgeable ground party to help beach the plane safely at the lake's edge at the end of each sortie.

When our turn came to fly, the reason for the Wellington boots became apparent. The process of getting in required sloshing around in the shallow water at the edge of the lake, before mounting the floats and transferring, not exactly gracefully, into the aircraft. After a bit of effort, I found myself secure in the rear seat, wondering quite what would happen next.

David started the engine and we were cast off and sailed off downwind. Once clear of the beach, David lowered the small water rudders at the rear of the floats and said "OK, you have control. Taxi slowly down to the far end of the lake."

This was definitely easier said than done.

Like any other aircraft, the vertical fin was designed to make the aircraft directionally stable in flight – so that it naturally stayed pointed more or less in the intended direction. Sat on the lake, with the tail surfaces pointed into wind, the opposite effect arose and the aircraft was directionally unstable and horribly difficult to steer.

The condition was made worse by the fact that the wind was pushing us at a fair rate and one could not use a blast of power to make the aerodynamic rudder effective. I thought that I would manage OK, as I was used to landing a tailwheel aircraft, which is also unstable directionally on the ground. I thought that I was doing pretty well until, when we were about two thirds of the way down the lake, the inevitable happened. There was a small deviation to the left; I applied full rudder to the right, but the water rudder was not effective enough to overcome the weather-cocking tendency of the fin. Quite slowly and gently, but with the determination of a dog chasing a rabbit, the aircraft continued to swing until it was facing into wind exactly in the opposite direction to our intended course. This was a bit humbling.

This is a water landing, so the wheels are ... up!

David said "I have control. Don't worry, that can happen to anyone on a windy day". He went on to explain that turning round on such a day was not a manoeuvre for the inexperienced. It required accelerating to the point where the aerodynamic controls were effective and then swinging around in a flat turn on the water.

"The outer wing will be moving quite a bit faster than the inboard wing, so you have to hold lots of opposite aileron in case the outer wing rises. If that happens, before you know what's happening, the wind will get under the wing, the inboard wingtip will hit the water and you'll be capsized in an instant".

We roared around the turn and ended up just about where we had started so that I could have a second try at taxying down the lake. This time, with lots of concentration and a better appreciation of the lag between applying the water rudders and seeing a steering response, I made it safely to the end and we let the aircraft swing back around into wind.

David put the flaps down to the take-off position and briefed me on the take-off procedure.

I was used to a tailwheel aircraft where, after opening the throttle you push the stick forward to raise the tail, thereby reducing the drag and allowing rapid acceleration along the runway.

As the speed increases, less forward stick is required to hold the aircraft level and, if properly trimmed, when it gets to the right speed, the aircraft will take-off, pretty much of its own accord.

"This time, when you open the throttle, you need to have the stick right back. The tail down attitude will help the floats to climb up their own bow waves and to start planing over the surface. The drag will then reduce dramatically and we'll accelerate away and fly off in the usual fashion".

Just exactly the opposite sequence to my normal technique!

David flew the first take off. I was quite impressed with the short run in the strong wind and also that the Super Cub had plenty of power to achieve a good climb rate two-up and with the extra drag of the floats.

Once the flaps were up, he passed control to me and we flew round the circuit.

He sat as best he could to one side so that I could see the airspeed indicator and talked me round onto the approach. We did the normal checks downwind, but when we were on short finals he said aloud "This is a ... water ... landing, so the wheels are ... up!"

Of course, there were no wheels on this occasion.

Had the aircraft been equipped with amphibious floats, which contain their own retractable undercarriage, we could in principle have been landing on either water, or on a hard runway.

In either case, having the wheels up when they should be down, or down when they should be up, gets very expensive, very quickly.

Consequently, this last configuration check on short finals is necessary whenever one is flying a float-equipped aircraft or a flying boat. With the wind streaks down the lake and the roughened surface, judging the direction and height for landing proved easier than I expected and I flew three circuits, each with a gentle touch down – very satisfying.

The most dangerous conditions for landing occur in 'glassy water' conditions, where the water is so still that there are no ripples or waves to provide a height reference.

One literally cannot tell where the surface lies.

Under these conditions, the technique is to set up an approach with a very slow descent rate (perhaps 100 foot per minute) and literally to wait until the floats find the surface before closing the throttle and raising the nose to slow down.

Having heard this described, I was quite pleased not to have to attempt it!

Hopefully, this little tale captures some of the challenges and differences encountered when messing about in seaplanes.

Heaven only knows what it is like on a fast-flowing river, or on the open sea with wind, waves and tide to contend with. It was tremendous fun and I am sure that I would have signed up to gain a Seaplane Rating.

Why didn't I?

Well, after its short season on floats, the aircraft returned to wheeled operations until the next summer.

Sadly, early in that second season it came to grief as a result of being capsized.

Somewhat ironically, and equally sadly, it was being flown by David Shepherd at the time; fortunately, he escaped wet, but entirely unhurt, from the upturned craft.

The opportunity to gain a Seaplane Rating had passed, but I had great fun and G-AVPT remains the only aircraft (so far) that I have flown whilst wearing Wellington boots.

Ron Smith

Chapter Ten

"On take-off we shall be using the afterburners for one minute and twenty-six seconds"

A flight in the iconic Concorde across the Atlantic to the world's biggest airshow.

Hilary and I visited the US Experimental Airplane Annual (EAA) Convention and Fly-In at Oshkosh in 1980. This event, which is now styled as AirVenture, attracts around 15,000 aircraft onto the same airfield for a week-long festival of flying that in turn attracts between 300,000 and 500,000 spectators.

Without question this is the place for the aircraft enthusiast. It's not just the mass formations of T-6 Texans, T-34s and Mustangs; the privately owned jets; the new designs; the mass of homebuilt aircraft; and the rare and obscure 'antiques'.

It's also the camaraderie, the workmanship and the showmanship which is irresistible.

US weather tends to extremes and on that occasion it was hot; temperatures in excess of 100F had been experienced somewhere in the lower 48 states on each of 30 consecutive days.

A massed formation of T-6 Texans joined by a couple of T-34 Mentors

Consequently, the daily weather forecast was generally "another severe clear" and Cessna wings were de rigeur as sunshades during the flying displays.

It was a great event and I remained for some time a member of the EAA, receiving their super magazine Sport Aviation with its outstanding photography, tales of jaw-droppingly beautiful restorations, stunning new designs and rear cover aviation artwork.

Concorde, that icon of Anglo-French engineering, has been something of a marker for my professional life.

I went to University to study Aeronautical Engineering in September 1969, just six months after the first British-built prototype made its maiden flight from Filton, the subject of a live and breathless commentary from Raymond Baxter.

A few months later I saw the aircraft ground running during a visit to the flight test centre at Fairford.

It was phenomenally noisy and produced an enormous plume of black smoke.

I left, not entirely convinced that it would ever see service.

Later, at Westland Helicopters, I worked with John Jupe, who had been the structural designer of the Concorde air intake system.

Ultimately I was able to have a private tour of the aircraft at its Heathrow maintenance facilities as part of a small group, just two weeks before the aircraft was finally withdrawn from service in October 2003.

In late 1984, my eye was caught by an advertisement saying, roughly: CONCORDE to Oshkosh; tour group forming to fly Concorde to Oshkosh; London – New York – Oshkosh by Concorde, return via TWA; target cost £1,300 round trip. This was extraordinary. At the time, BA had not yet polled their business customers to find out what they really thought a Concorde trip was worth, so this fare was just within reach. In fact in 1984, a round trip from London to New York cost £2,400, about a 30% premium on the First Class subsonic fare.

Later on, a survey of the most regular passengers, most of whom were leaders of industry and had little idea of their true travel costs, revealed that they valued the trip at least £5,000. BA was not slow in responding to this intelligence and by 2003, the round trip Concorde fare had increased to £8,230.

Whatever else, £1,300 for a round trip to Oshkosh looked hard to resist and after a hard think about the cost, we decided that I should take advantage of this value-for-money offer, which cannot have made much profit for either BA or TWA.

On the earlier Oshkosh visit, we had stayed at the University of Wisconsin and taken the bus to Wittman Field every day. The accommodation had been adequate, but a bit basic.

I made the same arrangement for this trip but, as we shall see, ended up staying elsewhere. At the time, I was working on a European four nation research project and sometime around March we had a study progress meeting in Munich. My friend (and customer), the late Alan Jones of RAE Farnborough, was with me and we headed out in the town centre looking for our evening meal. In the event, we walked into a warm, busy beer hall. It was not just busy – at first glance there seemed to be no seats available. We managed to find an empty table, but it was too good to be true; we sat down, but within minutes were moved on – apparently the table was reserved. By a stroke of good luck, we then managed to occupy a table for six by being in the right place, just as the previous guests rose to leave. This was literally the last table available. Perhaps, not surprisingly, we were joined shortly thereafter by a party of four Americans. Alan and I were talking about our summer plans. Alan was a keen sailor and RYA Yachtmaster Instructor and was due to take a party down to sail near the Channel Islands to experience the fast currents and high tides for which that area is famous.

"So, what are you up to?" he asked.

"Well, I'm off to Oshkosh to look at all the aircraft at the EAA Fly-In" I said, going on to explain how large the event was and what a tremendous experience it would be.

Concorde's iconic planform graces the skies

After a couple of minutes, the gentleman on my left turned to me and said "Gentlemen, I don't want you to think that we're listening to your conversation, but we come from Oshkosh! We don't often meet people in the US who have heard of the place, let alone who are going there. If you are coming to Oshkosh, you must stay with us".

We then had a very lively conversation. Tom and Kay Mettlach worked for the local High School, she as Librarian, he as Football Coach.

They would be on vacation at the time of the Fly-In, so "it would be no trouble at all". They spent a good deal of the evening trying to persuade Alan to come across at the same time and sail with them in their 26 ft sailboat on Lake Winnebago. They had always meant to go up through the lock system to the ocean that is Lake Michigan, but had never quite been brave enough to do so.

Tom and Kay insisted that I should have their address and phone number, which was duly written down on the back of one of my business cards.

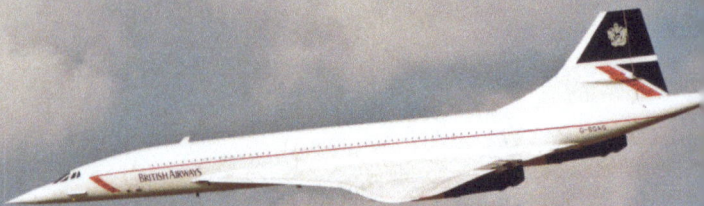

A few days before I was due to travel, and with some trepidation, I gave the Mettlachs a call. "You might not remember me, my name's Ron and we met in a beer hall in Munich. I thought that I'd let you know that I am indeed coming to Oshkosh, arriving on Saturday and that I have a room booked at the University".

The instant reply was "Hey, we've been waiting for your call. We'll cancel your room – you're staying with us".

This is the kind of open hearted generosity that speaks volumes of the nation and the individual.

Come the day of departure, I booked in through the dedicated Concorde Lounge and was duly shepherded onto the aircraft, G-BOAG.

To those of us accustomed to the modern wide-body fleet of Boeing 777s and Airbus 380s, cramped and small would probably be a reasonable first impression of the Concorde cabin.

The seats were of soft, grey leather and the service throughout was definitely First Class. Passengers were given a Concorde flight certificate signed by the crew, a model of the aeroplane and, of course champagne. One was also allowed, if not encouraged, to take home the individual bone china salt and pepper pots with their Concorde logos.

The pilot for this, the first appearance of Concorde at Oshkosh, was Capt John Cook. Later, John was to fight tenaciously to clear his son Richard's name after he, and his fellow pilot Jonathan Tapper, were unjustly found by an RAF enquiry to have been responsible for a dreadful Chinook accident in 1994 on the Mull of Kintyre. Sadly, John Cook did not live to see the crew fully exonerated in July 2011, with the MoD issuing a written apology to their families and relatives for the distress caused.

There was a more detailed pre-flight briefing from the crew than is normal, explaining that the aircraft would take off using afterburner – "On take-off we shall be using the afterburners for one minute and twenty-six seconds". The aircraft would then climb and accelerate to a high subsonic speed before again engaging afterburner, for a rather longer period, for the acceleration to supersonic flight. The cruise itself would not require afterburner. (Lockheed Martin refers to this as supercruise in the context of the F-22 Raptor and appears to think that it is something new).

It was also explained that the slender delta wing creates its lift at low speed by setting up two large leading edge vortices that create lift as they swirl over the wings (rather like the vortices that can be seen being formed by the leading edge strakes of an F-16 or F-18 in a high-g manoeuvre). Because these vortices tend to shift about somewhat unpredictably, the aircraft tends to shake a little at speeds below 250 kt.

The briefing was designed to ensure that this was an expected, rather than alarming, phenomenon.

The cruising altitude would be 58,000 ft at a Mach number of 2.02 (or about 1350 mph).

At a suitable point, there would be an opportunity for small groups of passengers to come up to the cockpit in supersonic cruise flight.

Concorde – a definitive combination of elegance, power and speed
Below: ... using the afterburner for one minute and twenty-six seconds

We pushed back, taxied and lined up. The aircraft was held on the brakes until full power was stabilised. On brake release, I was pushed back into my seat in a most satisfying fashion. There was an immense sensation of both power and acceleration and a marked subsequent reduction in both cabin noise and acceleration as the afterburner was cancelled exactly one minute and twenty-six seconds after brake release.

FLIGHT CERTIFICATE

Presented to

R.V. SMITH.

who flew supersonically on Concorde between LONDON & NEW YORK/OSHKOSH.

on 26ᵀᴴ JULY 1985.

Colin M. Marshall
Chief Executive

JOHN EAMES
Capt.

CONCORDE

John Jupe had told me that obtaining sufficient payload to carry 100 passengers transatlantic had been a significant challenge. Carbon fibre brakes had allowed the take-off weight to be increased by about 3,000 kg for the same runway length.

This may not sound a lot for an aircraft with a take-off weight of 92 tonnes, but it represents the weight of around 33 passengers, or one third of the total passenger load.

Concorde's maximum speed was limited by the strength of its Aluminium alloy structure at high temperatures. The temperature at the nose was some 127°C reducing to around 90°C over much of the fuselage outer skin.

The aircraft cruise Mach number had to be reduced (from an originally intended M2.2 to M2.02 after flight testing showed that significant and rapid changes of outside air temperature (temperature gradients) could be encountered at cruising altitude.

The reduced operating Mach number ensured that there could not be an inadvertent exceedence of airframe temperatures in flight. John had also said that due to the temperatures involved, the aircraft grew significantly in length in flight (by about nine inches, as I recall). The right hand edge of the Flight Engineer's instrument panel would be hard up against the cockpit bulkhead on the ground. In cruise, however, there would be a finger's width gap between the two – and there was. Certainly, one was conscious in the cruise that heat was radiating from the disappointingly small triple-glazed windows due to the external skin friction. The fact that the cabin was rather hot may have been due to optimising (in this case minimising) the amount of energy used for cabin environmental control, leaving the temperature warm, but just acceptable for a typical three hour Concorde flight.

Acceleration through the sound barrier took place over the South West Approaches to Britain and was completely routine, although the use of afterburner did give rise to a very evident increase in the cabin noise level.

One would not really have had any idea of the aircraft's speed or its cruise altitude, were it not for the large flight data display at the front of the cabin, showing in large green numerals the cruising height, the outside air temperature, speed (mph) and the Mach number. A visit to the slightly cramped cockpit confirmed the relatively poor view provided with the nose visor up and revealed an instrument panel full of relatively familiar electro-mechanical instrument dials.

The Flight Engineer station, looked, if anything, more complex than the pilots' flight instrument panel. The Flight Engineer monitored engine and intake parameters and the management of the fuel system, which included pumping fuel to and from a tank in the tail fin to maintain longitudinal balance in the different flight regimes.

We let down into Kennedy Airport to a grey, hazy sky, about an hour (local time) before our London departure time.

I fear that we were not too popular that day, as the late

Above: The instrument panel reveals Concorde's 1960s heritage

departure of a TriStar from the active runway meant that we performed a go around from low level at a late stage of the approach. The disturbance to the smooth ride due to the separated vortex flows was quite noticeable, but not at all disturbing. From New York, we made a high speed transit across to Wittman Field arriving in sunny weather to look down on a veritable sea of aircraft. Captain Cook set up the aircraft for the approach and we came whistling down to touch down moderately firmly. But, what's this? No deceleration! Then a roar from the afterburners as we performed a touch and go into a full airshow routine. The passengers could not have been more delighted. It was a perfect end to the flight of a lifetime. The flight back on TWA was also a flight to remember, for entirely different reasons, but that's another story.

Below: In-flight display M=2.01; 54,500 ft; -58C; 1,310 mph

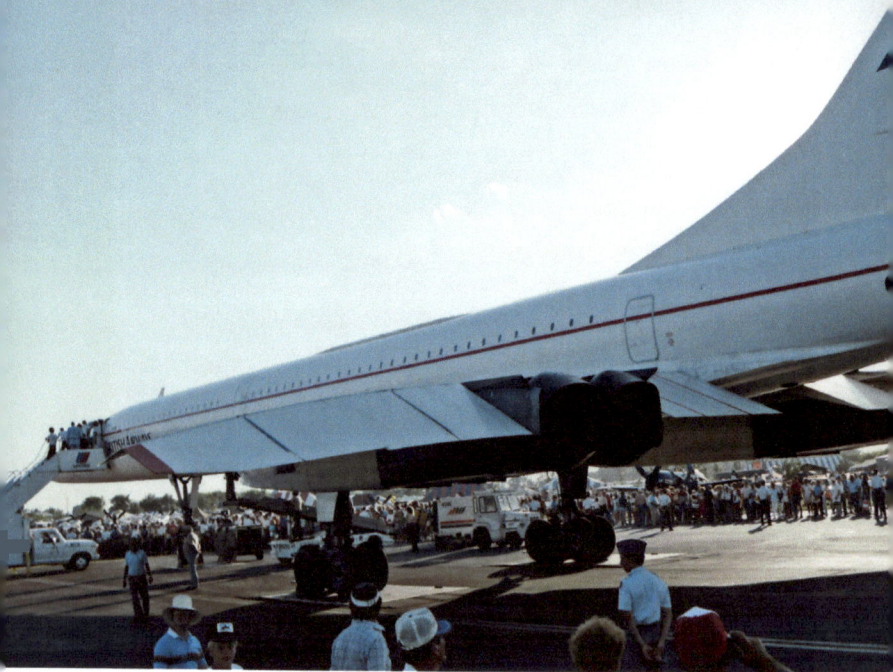
Concorde G-BOAG wowing the crowds at Oshkosh 1985

Below: Concorde and P51D Mustang – two iconic aircraft meet at Oshkosh

Above and Below Concorde   Right: The general aviation park on the Terminal side of the airfield with 5 DC-3s, a Beech 18 and numerous light aircraft

Above: A typical Oshkosh air show routine – wing-walking and aerobatics using a 450hp Stearman
Below: Oshkosh is famous for warbirds and immaculate restorations, exemplified by this Mustang

Above N2251D 'Miss Coronado' another superb example of the P-51 Mustang
Below Two Curtis P-40s on the flight line, the sort of rare sight that is almost unique to Oshkosh

Above: A rare and totally immaculate Douglas AD-1 Skyraider typifies the unique attractions of Oshkosh
Below: The Canadian Warbirds Heritage Mustang C-FFUZ

Above: A Grumman F-7F Tigercat
Below: The warbirds parking area with B-29, B-24, B-17 and numerous P-51s and T-28s

Schleicher K13 against a
Lasham cloudscape

Part 2
Lift is All
You Need

Ron Smith

Chapter Eleven
"Going for Solo"

A sailplane brings the pleasure of silent flight without an engine. Not having an engine brings its own special problems requiring a combination of skill and decision making not found in other forms of aviation.

In September 2009, I decided to invest a week's holiday in a gliding course at Lasham. I had flown a glider (if you can call a Cadet MkIII (or Tandem Tutor) a glider) in 1967. The three of us on the Lasham course flew on four of the five days.

The first flight was an aero-tow behind a 180hp Robin. A lot of concentration was required to hold position behind the tug in bumpy conditions.

It all settled down after the second try and I got into the syllabus proper, with lots of stalling and spinning. I lost count of how many we did; the spin entry from below 1,000ft certainly concentrated the mind (particularly as you end up low and at the wrong end of the airfield)!

One thing that you do learn is to recover pretty briskly – a short delay once the aircraft stops spinning and is pointed straight at the ground can get you up close and personal with the glider's never exceed speed limit in double-quick time.

I found winch launching much harder to get used to than I had remembered from my schooldays (off-putting acceleration and abnormally steep attitude). The upshot was that I had a pre-solo check ride (aerotow) on the last day of the course. That at least led to some real soaring and chasing another K13 glider round and round a thermal.

Ultimately, however, I didn't do a perfect approach, and they decided to give me one more low tow just to prove that I could really do it.

At the beginning of the week, I had asked if I could have a flight in a real high performance glider as all my previous experience had been on very low performance machines.

n as seen from a high-performance Schempp Hirth Nimbus 3DT

After I landed from the second solo check flight, I was told that I now had a choice between going solo or having a flight in a Nimbus 3DT. I chose the Nimbus.

Seven out of the top ten places in the 2009 British Nationals were taken by the Nimbus. It boasts around 80ft wingspan, has a glide ratio of 56:1 and is, I believe, worth of the order of €100k+. Its owner, Terry Salter, said he was happy to take passengers provided that they did some of the work. We ended up flying out and back from Lasham to Rivar Hill (southwest of Newbury). We flew for one and three quarter hours, mostly between 3,000 and 5,000 feet. Despite my best efforts, there was never any question of it not staying up. On return to Lasham, I was flying straight and level at 60 kts under a cloud street with the aircraft climbing steadily – 'solar powered flight', as I said to Terry.

Descending to join downwind, with the wheel down and airbrakes out, the glide angle was slightly better than for the K13 at its best. The upshot was that my 2009 gliding break did not see me flying solo.

In April 2010, I went on a 'Going for Solo' course at Bicester. On this course, the club provides an instructor for the week (£30 per day, no more than two students per instructor). Apart from being determinedly windy throughout, it was a pretty successful week.

It's hard to explain what it's like ... when it works and you are high enough to have time to relax (say above 3,000 ft), it's lovely. Otherwise, you are continually making decisions, whilst flying close to the stall as accurately as you can in a permanent practice forced landing (or, indeed, actual forced landing, as you have no ability to overshoot and try again).

On my first flight, we did an aerotow to see how I got on. We climbed up in a circle through a convenient hole in the cloud before casting adrift for "upper air work" – another code for spinning – followed by planning my own circuit to land. After the flight, the instructor asked me what I wanted to get out of the week. I said that I'd like to go solo and then see how far I got. His comment was "There is no question of you not going solo!"

I did a solo aerotow at the end of that first day; a solo winch launch on the second day; and was sent off solo in the K8 (single seater - photo) at the end of the third day. The K8 was more demanding, had a slower limit speed for winch launch and got bounced around more on the aerotow. It also lacked penetration in the windy conditions that prevailed all week. Flying a single seater that doesn't belong to you always adds a little more stress as well.

Perhaps the best illustration of the continuous decision making involved is given by a description of the pre-solo winch check-out, which involves a simulated cable break 'at an awkward height'. You sit in the glider, on your parachute (used on every flight) and complete your checks – CBSIFTCBE – Controls, Ballast, Straps, Instruments, Flying Controls, Trim, Canopy, Brakes, Eventualities (the latter being some positive thinking about 'what happens if …').

You signal for the cable to be attached and the wingman raises the wingtip. The crew signal the winch to take up slack and tension builds, literally and metaphorically, as you see the cable twitch, move and tauten. "All out" is signalled and then the fun begins. The V8 in the winch reels in the cable and the aircraft rushes forward. You are watching and ready for an instant release if the wing drops when the wingman lets it go.

The aircraft rises into the air and you look for at least 40 kts (the airspeed indicator needle is rushing around the dial). As soon as you see 40 you start to raise the nose (a determined and sustained pull is   required to keep the speed below 58kt in a K13, or rather less in a K8).

Your eyes flick from wing tip to wing tip so that you can check for any lateral drift in a crosswind. Your hand stays on the yellow cable release.

Suddenly there is a realisation that the acceleration has decreased and the airspeed is dropping.

A firm forward push to get the nose down and two quick pulls on the cable release. You keep pushing forward – the negative 'g' lifted my hat from my head. Pretty soon you get to what looks like the approach attitude. This is the dangerous part – a quick glance at the airspeed shows it is still less than 25 kt. You have to wait for 50 to 55 kts before starting to manoeuvre.

After an age (say 4 or 5 seconds) the speed recovers. Next decision – is there room to land ahead. Answer – no! This is an 'awkward height' failure, after all.

You turn in the pre-planned direction (to starboard in this case). Is there room for an abbreviated circuit and land into wind? No – this is an 'awkward height' failure after all.

2009 at Bicester: solo in a glider for the first time since 1967 and cleared to fly the single seat Schleicher K8b

You fly downwind 'far enough' and then, having picked an intended landing point, turn in crosswind and pull out about half airbrake at the appropriate point. It is then a question of speed control and crabbing crosswind to just the right point to kick off the drift and land.

I got a bit fast in the turn and was a bit further into the field than I planned, but my instructor said – "An absolute textbook demonstration", which was pleasing.

I find a little gliding goes a long way in terms of improved flying skills, judgement and decision making.

Having said that, getting back to the field, when you've drifted that little bit further downwind than you intended, can be distinctly 'creepy'. I still remain a strictly trainee glider pilot, but I can heartily recommend the experience of 'Going for Solo'.

Jim Smith

Chapter Twelve
"All Aircraft Bite Fools"

A tale of schoolboys, bicycles, old aircraft and the days before airport security had been invented.

Well, what would you expect of twins at boarding school? Trouble and lots of it, pretty much all of the time.

First of all, we had spent three years of adventure and mischief in Guyana (then British Guiana), and were about as far away from the British Public School culture as you could be. Secondly, you could never tell which of us was responsible for any misdemeanour, because we were identical, and it always seemed to be 'the other one'.

After a while, the school simply assumed 'both'. Independent, disobedient and lively – and moreover, bright enough to realise that if the first story was completely unbelievable, the second story, though equally untrue, was quite likely to be believed – just so long as it was just a little more plausible.

We were at boarding school because we had run out of the Guyanese education system. But we were in enough trouble that when the holidays came around we needed to have a serious talking to.

Well, I can't say we reacted all that well to a talking to – we'd had a few of those at school, but when Uncle Robert, instead of just telling us off, started talking instead about finding hobbies to keep us out of mischief, he captured our interest.

He worked in the light aircraft insurance business, and he had all these photos of slightly distressed (and sometimes very distressed) aircraft to show us and to talk about. The interest he sparked has turned into an enduring passion for aircraft, for photography and for flying that has lasted nearly 50 years.

The first steps down this path came from the realisation that at Caterham School, we weren't all that far (well about 11 miles) from Gatwick airport, and there were other airfields not too far away – Biggin Hill and Kenley, key fighter airfields in the Battle of Britain, and Redhill, then home of The Tiger Club and full of interesting machines and exciting flying.

British United Carvair 'Menai Straits' in the General Aviation area at Gatwick

Above: A Dan Air Airspeed Ambassador photographed 'through the fence'

Below: Charrington United Breweries bottle-green Piaggio 166 G-ARUJ

At school, we knew about Kenley, because the school's Air Training Corps cadets had parades there, and went gliding. Biggin Hill, we knew, had occasional air shows and we could see aircraft operating from either Redhill or Gatwick from the aptly named 'Viewpoint' a short distance away to the south east of the school on the edge of the North Downs.

On Saturday and Sunday afternoons, we had free time at school, and could go for 'walks'. We had classes on Saturday mornings and compulsory church on Sunday mornings. Time was limited – what could we do?

Well, the England of 1964 was very different from the England of today.

The roads were relatively quiet, and we had earlier discovered that hitch-hiking was a possibility. This had much to do with family holidays from Northampton when the family motorbike and sidecar (!) would nearly always break down on a long trip

…In fact father used to say it broke down every time it travelled on the A1, in other words, at every opportunity.

As a hobby, we conceived the idea of visiting the airfields and photographing any old or unusual aircraft we came across, and making these pictures into a display for the annual Hobby Competition. Looking back on the pictures of the time, one is struck by two main aspects. Firstly, the extraordinary access to aircraft available at the airport, in terms of viewing galleries offering rooftop access above the aircraft stands, and secondly, the remarkable access that two lads on bicycles could achieve at small airfields like Biggin and Redhill and even at Gatwick.

At Gatwick, Dan Air was flying the Airspeed Ambassador, the Bristol Freighter, and the Comet. British United Airlines were still operating the Dakota, alongside the Handley Page Herald, Britannia and the VC10. A range of European and American charter operators and airlines including operating types such as the DC-6, and DC-7, and the occasional Constellation.

Above: One could often see rare and unusual types at Gatwick, in this case McKinnon Turbo-Goose G-ASXG
Below: The Tiger Club was home of both aerobatic and vintage aircraft; this is the sole surviving Arrow Active

A variety of relatively rare jet and turbo-prop aircraft, including the Convair Coronado, the Caravelle, Tupolev 104, Ilyushin 18 and Canadair CL-44 could also be seen.

At Redhill, the collection of vintage aircraft operated by the Tiger Club was always of interest, complemented by helicopters from far-flung regions of the globe operated by Bristow Helicopters, and a number of prototypes built or flown at the airfield. The variety was stunning, and the flying was equally spectacular. The sight of Neil Williams, a great and sadly-missed flyer of the time, streaking inverted across the airfield in the tiny Cosmic Wind 'Ballerina', with the tailfin perhaps 10 ft above the grass is an enduring memory.

The main aircraft of the club were the Tiger Moth, the French Stampe SV4, and the Rollason-built Turbulent. But these were supplemented by the tiny Cosmic Wind, and Luton Beta racing aircraft; the vintage Fox Moth and Arrow Active; the exotic Alaparma Baldo from Italy; and Jodel touring aircraft such as the Mousquetaire and Mascaret, for which Norman Jones of Rollason's / the Tiger Club was UK agent.

For all those aircraft stressed to the appropriate limits, aerobatics was de rigeur, and many a happy visit was spent watching Stampe, Tiger Moth, Cosmic Wind, Zlin and on one occasion Charles Masefield's visiting P-51 Mustang, performing and practising aerobatic routines. As 'harmless boys', we were able to walk out on to the airfield and look at the aircraft; touch them; smell the warm oil smell that comes with aircraft like the Tiger Moth; and even listen to the ticking noises as the Merlin engine of the Mustang gently cooled in the summer evening air. Looking at the Tiger Club aircraft, despite their variety, we could see they all had one thing in common. In the cockpit of every aircraft, high up on the instrument panel where it would be in the scan pattern for the key instruments, a small white placard carrying the words

"ALL AIRCRAFT BITE FOOLS"

Inscribed in red letters. A message as sound today, as it was fifty years ago - is still carried by all aircraft of the Tiger Club.

Above: Hiller 12E4 of Bristow Helicopters landing at Redhill
Below: Regular RCAF visitors to Gatwick included the Douglas C-47, Bristol Freighter and Canadair Yukon

Above: The early fleet of British United included this Douglas DC-3, seen in the maintenance area
Below: Adria Airways - another of the small charter airlines flying the Douglas DC-6 out of Gatwick

A typically diverse selection within the Tiger Club Hangar, A shark-toothed Alaparma Baldo 75 in the company of a Chrislea Super Ace, two Turbulents, an Autocar, a Jodel and a Fox Moth

JODEL DR 1050

N'378

Above: Among the less-than-familiar airlines to be seen was Ariana Afghan Airlines, in this case operating a Douglas DC-6 Below: British United was a launch customer for the BAC One Eleven

Above: The diminutive Levier Cosmic Wind G-ARUL 'Ballerina' was flown by Neil Williams in the World Aerobatic Championships   Below: Percival Q6 G-AFFD was a long-term resident in the Chelsea College of Aeronautics hangar at Redhill

A rare Procaer F15B Picchio seen outside the maintenance hangars at Gatwick

Above: The one-off Storey TSR3 Wonderplane
Below: A Bristol Freighter still in use with Dan Air

Above: The one-off Storey TSR3 Wonderplane was flown at Redhill sporting a Union Jack colour scheme on its upper surfaces Below: Zlin 526 Trener G-AWAR landed by Neil Williams in a display of outstanding airmanship after suffering a wing spar failure in flight while practising for the 1970 World Aerobatic Championships

Another typically busy Tiger Club hangar scene including
- a Turbulent,
- the TSR3 Wonderplane,
- the Arrow Active,
- two Jodels,
- a Centre Est Regent
- and a Tiger Moth, with a second Tiger outside on the airfield

Lift off in' Spotnik'

Ron Smith

Chapter Thirteen
"The trouble with Inflation"

Ballooning is an addictive form of aviation where local weather, terrain, hot air, electricity pylons, farmers and livestock conspire to make an apparently peaceful activity full of excitement and challenges.

Ballooning is an incredibly social activity; the flight crew is completely dependent on the ground crew both to get in the air and to get retrieved. Flying takes place in the early morning before wind gusts and thermals can get going, or in the early evening as it all calms down again. There is a delightful tendency for early flights to end with a cooked breakfast and evening flights to adjourn to the pub.

Hilary and I were invited into balloon crewing when one of Hilary's work colleagues, Lucy, asked if we would be interested in becoming a reserve crew for their balloon. The instant answer - yes, we'd be delighted.

Lucy's husband, Brian, was a qualified balloon pilot (or possibly aeronaut, on the assumption that the term does not solely apply to gas balloons). They owned a Cameron V77 G-BMHK, for which Lucy had designed the canopy – red with black spots - and known as 'Spotnik'. Erecting and inflating a hot air balloon is, at first, a pretty scary business.

One has to load gas bottles into the basket and connect them to the burner assembly. The canopy is laid out flat on the ground and the basket, tipped on its side, is connected via a few slender lift cables.

When we first started, the next part of the procedure was to don some heat-protective gloves and flap the envelope's base to try to get a reasonable volume of air into it. At this stage, the balloon is laying semi-flattened on the ground, looking as if someone had left behind an enormous party balloon, that has had four or five days to lose most of its pressure.

The fun really begins now; two of the crew are deputed to hold the neck of the balloon as far open as possible, while the pilot ignites the burners and directs the roaring crackling flame into the opening. The flame passes seemingly far too close to the crew members' hands in the process.

Gradually the warm air starts to both lift and inflate the balloon, which needs to be steadied by a head rope, so that it remains stable as it stands up. Being a dedicated coward, that was the job for me!

Later on, health and safety became more of a consideration and a petrol driven fan with guarded, cropped blades was used to blow cold air at a high rate into the balloon, prior to burner ignition. This was such an effective and simple device; one wondered why it had taken so long to come into use. Brian and Lucy were great fun and once we were reasonably competent, the whole process became far less daunting.

The highlights of our all-too-brief sojourn as balloon crew included some very amusing incidents.

Our first passenger flight took place after a hot summer day.

We took off from North Cadbury Court in the company of another balloon, flown by Archie Montgomery, whose family produce Montgomery Cheddar – some of the best cheese in the land.

The two balloons proceeded in company, making a spectacular sight in the evening light.

As we progressed, it became apparent that, after such a warm day, land breezes were setting in, meaning that the wind speed was increasing, rather than dropping as evening approached. Brian gave a quick radio call to Lucy in the retrieve car "I promise that we won't fly off the edge of the map". We promptly flew off the edge of the map! We were rapidly approaching the Bournemouth-Southampton controlled airspace and encountering a succession of unsuitable landing fields. Conscious of the need to get on the ground pretty soon, we flew over a line of trees, beyond which there was a large open field, albeit with a high tension electricity line beyond.

"Hold on tight and keep your knees bent, this will be a heavy landing. I can't risk drifting on towards those wires. Make sure that whatever happens, you don't fall out". We landed fast and with a big thump. The basket tipped on its side and dragged at speed across the stubble. Despite the warning, I was nearly shot out of the basket and was bodily pulled back in. We came to rest with a few grazes and began tidying up to speed up the retrieve. Brian subsequently gave us our Balloon First Flight Certificates, suitably amended to read First Crash Certificate.

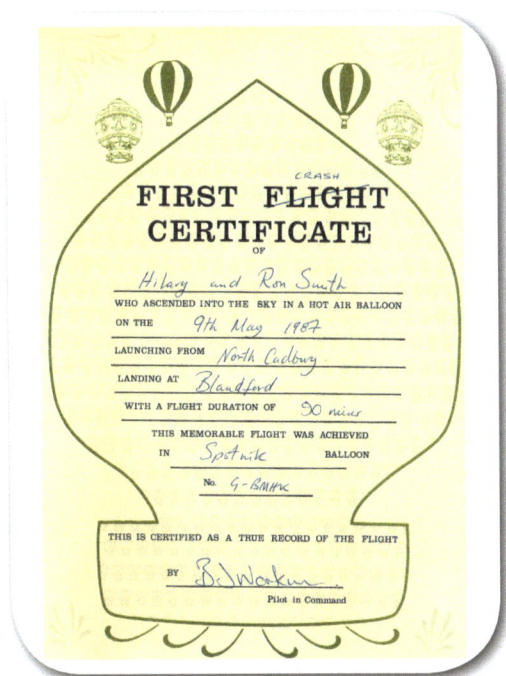

FIRST ~~FLIGHT~~ CRASH
CERTIFICATE
OF

Hilary and Ron Smith
WHO ASCENDED INTO THE SKY IN A HOT AIR BALLOON
ON THE 9th May 1987
LAUNCHING FROM North Cadbury
LANDING AT Blandford
WITH A FLIGHT DURATION OF 90 mins
THIS MEMORABLE FLIGHT WAS ACHIEVED
IN Spotnik BALLOON
No. G-BMHK

THIS IS CERTIFIED AS A TRUE RECORD OF THE FLIGHT
BY B J Workman
Pilot in Command

We had a flight in another balloon taking off from the stately home at Barrington Court. On this occasion, speculation about the actual cloud base resulted in a climb to no less than 10,500 ft, at which height, the face blew off Hilary's watch. A certain amount of nerve is required to remain comfortable in a creaking wicker basket, held on by thin cables to a fabric envelope, when nearly two miles up.

Brian and Lucy were incredibly active flyers, achieving up to 100 hours in a season, something I have never got close to doing in a powered aircraft, despite it being theoretically far less weather-sensitive than a balloon. This enthusiasm extended to flying whilst Lucy was eight months and three weeks pregnant. It was, admittedly, a perfect day, on which the Spotnik photo at the start of this piece was taken.

Hilary and I were acting as ground crew and the balloon slowly drifted south toward the Somerset levels, to the point where we ended up on the very last road from which you could access the moor. I was driving Brian's Cortina Estate with the balloon trailer behind and I had virtually no experience of towing a trailer.

We drove down the narrow lane to the landing site and guessed that the field entrance would be at the top of the field – wrong!

I ended up trying to negotiate a tight turn into the lower access lane and getting the car stuck hedge-to-hedge across the road. Just as I attempted the umpteenth reverse manoeuvre, the gear lever became completely detached and literally 'came off in my hand'.

Hilary ran down the lane to let Brian and Lucy know why it was taking so long for us to appear. When she came back, she was laughing; she had found them in their own pickle. For the first and only time, there had been no wind at all when they pulled the rip to collapse the balloon. As a result, the whole lot had come down on top of the basket, from which they were disentangling themselves with some merriment when Hilary arrived.

Our last experience ballooning was to crew for Archie's craft, which was being flown by Brian, to waft a newly married couple away from their wedding reception. Archie had taken the contract, forgetting that it clashed with a rugby tour in France that he was also committed to.

We hid the retrieve vehicle behind an outbuilding out of sight of the reception marquee. The wind was a little strong and there was a fairly tense discussion with the best man as to what was the latest time we could fly with a reasonable prospect of the best man being able to get the couple to the airport in time for their flight.

Ultimately, Brian decided that the breeze was falling sufficiently to allow us to launch. His exact instructions were: "You all know what you are doing, so I want it to look professional. No running about shouting at each other". He must have been roughly right, because we had the balloon rigged, inflated, and upright with its passengers installed ready for launch, within ten minutes.

When Brian and I went back to pick up Archie's portable inflating fan, the wedding guests were highly delighted and did their best to persuade us to join the party!

Archie Montgomery's balloon photographed from 'Spotnik' flying over Sutton Montis

Ron Smith

Chapter Fourteen
"Don't Pick any Wrong 'Uns'"

A story of working at London's Heathrow airport before there were high fences and all airliners looked the same.

"OK lads, what do you know about crack testing?" The short answer was not a lot. It was August 1970 and Jim and I were working as a holiday job at an executive jet maintenance organisation at Heathrow Airport. The pay was strictly nominal and just enough to cover costs, including digs in Hounslow, meals and travel to work.

The job had come about through some string-pulling by our Uncle Robert, on the basis that we were hard-working and enthusiastic and would benefit from seeing any interesting processes or activities that arose during our short stay with the firm. Crack testing fell into this category and we were given a quick demonstration of dye penetrant and magnetic particle testing.

Whichever method was used, it was obvious that you needed a disciplined approach and sharp eyesight to obtain reliable results. It turned out that the reason for the task was the need to fit a new brake drum to a de Havilland Heron.

At some time in the long lost past, a batch of drums had been produced that proved prone to cracking around their attachment bolts. Consequently this awkward, heavy, barrel-shaped object needed to be tested and shown to be free from cracks before being fitted.

That completed, and with the aircraft jacked up, we faced another hard ball question from the inspector. "How do you think that you'll get the old drum out of the wheel?"

The Shell Heron awaits its new brake drums

The cast iron brake drum sits tightly within a magnesium wheel hub, the disparity between the stiffness of the two materials meaning that one cannot apply a tool or lever to the drum without risking damaging the hub.

The answer proved to be a trick of the trade. Three men lifted the wheel and tyre and held it horizontally at about eighteen inches above the hangar floor.

On the command "three, two, one ... drop!" the whole assembly was dropped with a satisfying clang onto the hangar floor. On picking up the wheel, there was the brake drum, the source of the clang, sitting on the hangar floor.

The answer to the question was therefore a combination of inertia and conservation of momentum.

The company was maintaining a number of aircraft against their respective scheduled maintenance schedules. After a quick test of our ability to secure and wire lock some hydraulic pipe unions, our working week normally started with jacking up a Hawker Siddeley HS 125 and implementing a hydraulic line modification. I think that we were both aware of the trust that was being placed on us, given the value of the aircraft and our general lack of experience.

During our stay, we learned how to measure the tension in the flight control cables – this involved taking up access panels in the cabin floor and applying a device that measured how much force was required to deflect the cable by a fixed amount when supported between two fulcrum points. Another case of 'it's easy, when you know how'.

On another day, we were preparing an aircraft for the scheduled fungal inspection of its fuel tanks – an aircraft equivalent of a between-the-toes inspection for athlete's foot. It was definitely a surprise to me that fungus can grow in aircraft fuel tanks, but apparently it can, particularly in warm conditions and with any water present in the fuel. Every so often, one has to look for it.

Above: A Douglas DC-3 of Welltrade – possibly one of the last of its type to visit Heathrow
Below: Hawker Siddeley HS 125 outside the maintenance hangar

Above: Fairchild C-82 'Ontos' landing with engine spares for TWA
Below: Another rare Heathrow visitor, Beech 18 N15750. Two different Beech 18s visited whilst we were working there

This means draining the fuel (as far as possible) and then removing the plates covering the under-wing inspection panels. Like almost everything connected to aircraft maintenance, this is harder than it sounds.

It was definitely a case of "Oh, Yuck!" as the delicately fragranced and oily kerosene ran down my arm. I kicked the nearby bucket into place under the dribbling inspection access of the HS125 as the unusable / undrainable fuel ran out of the under-wing fuel tank access panels. We then retreated to wash the stinking fuel off and have a cup of tea.

The fuel tanks on the 125 are integral to its wing structure, and consequently, the inspection covers are solid load-bearing plates, secured by a ring of high torque fasteners, themselves additionally held solidly in place by three or four coats of glossy white exterior paint.

Each fastener was screwed firmly into the wing structure, but was provided with a small Allen key aperture in its centre for 'easy' removal.

That is to say that their removal may well have seemed easy to the aircraft designer sat at his desk, rather than grovelling on a hangar floor being dripped upon with fuel. In practice, the process began with the use of a dental tooth pick to clear paint from the circumference of each individual fastener and its central aperture.

One then inserted the Allen key in an attempt to free the fastener. The normal success rate seemed to be about 70%, but Jim seemed to be particularly diligent in his preparations and only about 10% of his fasteners needed to be drilled out using a pneumatically driven drill.

Working at Heathrow was not all about tricky, not to say, impossible, tasks.

The management and fellow workers were friendly and tolerant of our occasional mistakes.

They were, if anything, rather bemused by the thought that a pair of aeronautical engineering students would actually want to get their hands dirty working on real aircraft.

These were happy and unthreatening days at Heathrow, with only three terminals in use and a pleasing variety of aircraft, large and small. The smaller visiting aircraft used to park close by and at lunchtime it would be possible to nip out and catch the odd photograph.

Visitors that I remember included a Beagle 206 of The Steam Chicken Line, two Beech 18s, a DC-3 of Welltrade and early Gulfstream 2s. When was the last time a Beech 18 landed at Heathrow?

Inside the hangar, the aircraft were also owned by operators that are redolent of their times.

The HS125 owners included Busy Bee of Norway and Green Shield Stamps. Perhaps the rarest visitor that we saw was the infrequent coming and going of the TWA Steward-Davis C-82 Jet Packet N9701F 'Ontos' that would waddle off after landing to the cargo area, presumably with urgently needed spare parts.

We walked around the perimeter (no cars in those student days) all the way to the Perry Vale works (roughly from the present Terminal 4, which had not yet been built, to the present Terminal 5, which had not even been thought of), to photograph the decaying remains of Canadair Argonaut G-ALHJ.

Also, the firm put us in an aircraft tow truck for a trip through the cargo tunnel, which runs from the south to north side of the airport under the runway, to see up close a Pan Am Boeing 747. 1970 was the first year of service of the type, so it was still very much a novelty.

Almost unbelievably, it would seem that our presence actually contributed to the scheduled programme of work being finished ahead of time.

Rather than have us hanging around on a Friday afternoon, obviously under-employed, the management would put us in the cockpit of an HS125 (to operate the parking brakes) and tow us onto a general aviation stand in the middle of the airport.

Above: The decaying Argonaut at Perry Vale – underneath the present Terminal 5

We were then left to look after the aircraft and generally take in the scene, until they came to pick us and the aircraft up at the end of the day.

Thus it was on Friday 28th August 1970, we saw the performer Tiny Tim and a lady friend board a Piper Aztec en route to the Isle of Wight pop festival, where he was performing the following day.

Looking out from our hangar vantage point, we would often see large mushrooms growing on the grass beyond the company apron. Lunchtime would often provide an opportunity to pick a few, which our landlady would fry up for us at breakfast the next day.

More often than not, however, a gang mower would appear and shred the lot before we could get to them.

There was also a rumour that either the Airport Fire Service or Police had a franchise on the picking of the mushrooms. In those days before the general paranoia about terrorist threats at airports became commonplace, the airfield itself was separated from the perimeter road by a three rail wooden fence, of the type that one might expect to see around the garden of a largish private house in the country to stop stock wandering into the grounds.

One evening after work, before heading back to our digs, we had gone through the fence and were picking mushrooms on the 'infield' so to speak.

Inevitably, we attracted the attention of the airport police.

"What are you doing?" they said.

Tiny Tim and party en route to the Isle of Wight pop festival

"Picking mushrooms", we replied.

They then asked how was it that we were on the airfield, inside the fence.

"We work here"

After a further discussion to enquire who exactly we were working for and to ask the name of our manager, the police lost interest and left us to it, with the parting shot "Don't pick any wrong 'uns". There is something to be said for those rather more relaxed days before photo-IDs and razor wire.

Ron Smith

Chapter Fifteen

"I Can Manage the Signature"

This way to obtain travel documents is not recommended, even if you are an identical twin. Then, it could be managed with good humour; now there would probably be severe consequences.

By 1971, we had worked for three firms in the UK and the chance came up, again through our Uncle Robert, for the opportunity to work in an aircraft factory in Germany.

This was organised with the help of Brian Stevens and Neil Jensen, who were directors of Sportair Ltd, the UK agents of Sportavia Putzer Gmbh of Dahlemer Binz, in the German Eifel Mountains.

The company was building the RF4 and RF5 motor gliders (and related types such as the RF5B Sperber, SFS31 and RF7) and the Scheibe SF 25 Motorfalke, as well as servicing earlier types such as the Putzer Elster.

The necessary administrative arrangements were made in the background, and we duly received letters inviting us to work at Sportavia for three weeks during the Easter holidays.

This was, itself, contingent upon us getting the necessary paperwork in order in time to catch a free flight to Germany in the Sportair-owned Jodel D140 Mousquetaire G-ARLX.

Above: Sportair's Jodel D140 photographed at Biggin Hill before flying to Dahlemer Binz
Below: G-ARLX parked in the summer sun at Thruxton

The paperwork involved a visit to the visa section of the West German Embassy (then in Holborn) to fill in the necessary forms, which turned out to be for a work permit and residence permit. As it happened, I could not attend with Jim on the day, due to a University commitment. Jim's tale of the encounter at the Embassy goes something like this:

Having got to meet with the relevant clerk and exchanged the normal pleasantries the clerk asked "How can I be of assistance?"

"I'd like to take up an offer of a holiday job in Germany and don't know what's required"

"Is this a student exchange, or an offer of employment?"

Jim said that it was an offer of employment – we were aware, even in those pre-internet days that a student exchange would have required demonstrating a working knowledge of German, which we did not possess.

"Have you got an offer letter from an employer?" He had.

"For the residence permit, you will have to fill in a form and provide a valid passport and two passport photos; you may need a medical certificate"

"Can you please fill in these forms?" The official passed across a sheaf of paper.

Jim had just one more question "As you can see from the letter, the job offer is also for my brother. Can I fill in a form for him as well?"

The official said "Not really. He is supposed to be here himself. What about the signature on the form?"

Jim's account of the encounter goes on: I looked him in the eye and said disarmingly "I can manage the signature!"

Surprisingly, this did not result in his being thrown out on his ear. The official said "That's all very well, but what about the photograph?"

This gave Jim the perfect opportunity to explain that we were identical twin brothers and looked indistinguishable from each other. "I'll give you two photos of myself with the glasses on, and two with the glasses off" he offered.

… After a pregnant pause, the official smiled and said "OK!"

Now, even I would doubt that this was entirely true, were it not for the fact that we went back to Germany in the summer. This time we knew that we should both go to the Embassy, which we duly did. Evidently the same visa clerk was on duty, because as we walked in he said "Oh, Mr Smith, I do enjoy it when you come here, it livens up the day! … Oh, you are similar, aren't you!"

This time they got the right signatures, but two photos of me with the glasses on and two with the glasses off. (Photo-Me passport photo booths gave you as strip of four photos, and this was both quicker and cheaper for us than separately paying for more photos than we actually needed). We again caught our flights for a ten-week working summer at Dahlemer Binz.

The next summer, we came unstuck. This was the long summer holiday after completion of our first degrees – we were both staying on for post-graduate qualifications and had no immediate need to look for permanent employment.

We had the job offer and the flight arranged and submitted all the paperwork.

VISAS

Reg. No.: _1510_   Gebühr - Fee - Frais : _£1.15_

AUFENTHALTSERLAUBNIS
Residence Permit - Autorisation de séjour
(Sichtvermerk — Visa)

für die Bundesrepublik Deutschland einschl. des Landes Berlin
for the Federal Republic of Germany including the Land Berlin
pour la République Fédérale d'Allemagne y compris le Land Berlin

für
for   Familienname - Surname - Nom de famille
pour

          Vornamen - Christian names - Prénoms

vom   bis zum
from   till   _21. Juni 197_
à partir du   jusqu'au

Erteilt mit Zustimmung der Ausländerbehörde in
Issued with the approval of the aliens' authority in
Délivrée après autorisation par l'autorité pour les étrangers à

K. Scheider

          2 2. MRZ. 1971

London   Datum:

Behörde: **Botschaft**
          der
Bundesrepublik Deutschland

Unterschrift

Nur zur Arbeitsaufnahme

bei : _Fa. Pützer & Co. GmbH_

in : _Schmidtheim Eifel Flugplatz_

This time, we thought that the Embassy deserved to get two photos of each of us.

The only problem was that we again did this by paying for a single strip and this time rapidly swapping over between the second and third photographs. The problem was that we were similarly dressed and forgot to separate the photos into two pairs.

There was a long delay waiting for the return of the passports and we missed our free flights to Germany.

Eventually, the passports were returned, with a note to the effect that "We are sorry for the delay in processing your application, but you seem to have sent us four photographs of the same person!"

A great shame, but it does show that when you have a plan that works, changing it is not always a good idea.

Below: A repainted G-ARLX at the delightful Compton Abbas airfield

Ron Smith

Chapter Sixteen

"Would anyone like to play a game of Nim?"

A holiday job working in the small aircraft factory of Sportavia Putzer at Schmidtheim in Germany provides the backdrop for this tale of aeronautical and social fun.

When we arrived in Dahlemer Binz, we were looked after by the Site General Manager, who took us down to the centre of Schmidtheim to the guest house that he had arranged that we should stay in.

He had a very considerate discussion with the landlady, to ensure that we were able to settle in, given our general lack of spoken German. This even extended to asking her to make sure that we got to know some of the young people in the village and so it was that when we sat down to eat our first evening meal, we found ourselves joined by two very attractive girls, Birgit and Michaela, who were slightly younger than we were.

This was a brilliant move, as the girls made sure that we got to know other young people in the village and were included lots of local events.

We also made use of the pub opposite, which sold Bitburger Pils; each drink being marked by a pen stroke on the beer mat; it was definitely a good evening if you needed to start on the second (i.e. underside) of the mat. The cellar was used as a disco and I have an abiding memory of a tall youth dancing in a crash helmet to protect his head from the low ceiling.

The Rolling Stones were very popular, and it appeared that Michaela was known as 'Kleine Königin" (Little Queenie) after the Stones / Chuck Berry song.

On another occasion, we were in the cellar and there was a French lad there who could not speak German. Jim did a sterling job of translating German to broken French and French to broken German.

This was remarkably successful and had the unexpected result that thereafter, whenever we met a certain girl in the street, she would wave and call "Hallo, Franzosen" (Hello, Frenchmen) and laugh.

There was a pinball machine in the bar and my assumption that there was no real skill in pinball was rapidly dispelled by the owner's son, who appeared to be about five or six years old.

He would tow a bar stool over to the machine and clamber up it to reach the machine. He would then proceed to win multiple free replays, making the whole thing looked trivially easy ... until, of course, you tried it yourself!

Humiliation at pinball, put us in mind of a game called Nim, which had been shown to us once by a smug Frenchmaster at school. A series of matches are laid out in a triangle – one match in the top row, two in the next and so on to a final row of five matches.

The rules of the game are that each player removes a number of matches from any single row in turn, the aim being to force your opponent to take the last match. It sounds deceptively simple, but in practice, you can only win if you know what you are doing.

We sat on the beds in the guest house and went through all the moves of the game: "If I do that ... what do you do?" until we knew exactly how you won and why it was such a difficult game to work out if you'd not seen it before. Once we were pretty confident, we headed to the bar and showed our German friends the game. We played and lost a few times before suggesting that we play the next time for a beer.

The German psyche is attracted by the thought that there must be a rule or structure to determine the outcome and as a result, they were desperate to work it out and win.

So successful was this ploy, that after a while, all we had to do was to walk into the bar, shake a box of matches and ask "Does anyone fancy a game of Nim?" for someone to simply buy us a beer, rather than play the game.

At the weekends and summer evenings, we had a fantastically friendly, fun time filled with swimming, going to the local festivals (Kirmes and Jägerfest in the various local villages). One day, we decamped in two small BMWs into the countryside. After parking in an isolated field, the party walked over a wooded hillside and then sat down on a sunny bank to watch, without tickets, sports car racing at the Nürburgring.

Our jobs at the airfield were quite varied.

I spent some time installing engines in Scheibe Motorfalkes, learning just how difficult it was to secure the propeller bolts by wire locking them in pairs. I also made clamping plates to hold the top end of the underwing outriggers for the RF5, cutting thick Aluminium with an un-guarded band saw.

Jim meanwhile was assisting with wing construction and producing 'storchklappenkasten' – boxes for the wing-mounted airbrakes. The friendly workforce wanted to practice their English, so we agreed that they would, as far as possible, speak to us in English, whilst we would, as far as possible reply in German – a certain amount of hilarity ensued.

Together, we checked the English in the RF5 flight manual and then proceeded to translate the RF5 parts list from first principles. This was a bit tricky as one had to find an accurate and meaningful description of each component in no more than about three words. At times, we resorted to obtaining individuals items from the stores and then working our way through the production aircraft until we found the point where the particular part was fitted; this was usually enough to allow us to grasp the part's function.

Dahlemer Binz was a lovely grass airfield in the Eifel Mountains at 1900 ft above sea level, whose main use, apart from the Sportavia factory, was as a gliding site; it now has a tarmac runway and has become quite a modern airport, although it still retains its gliding operations.

A range of interesting aircraft would come and go and, if possible, we would nip onto the airfield at lunchtime to photograph any interesting visitors.

Typically, there would be occasional visits from Dornier Do27s in military service; Putzer Elster aircraft, which were still supported by the factory; and other light aircraft.

Probably the most unusual visitor was the sole Aachen FVA18 Primitivkrahe (primitive-crow), a low powered and angular high wing aircraft, whose appearance was well-suited to its name.

The unique Aachen FVA18 Primitivkrahe

The factory itself was busy producing the RF4 and RF5 one and two seat motor gliders and the SFS-31 which was a marriage between the RF4 and the Scheibe SF27 sailplane, having RF4 fuselage and SF27 wings.

During our time there, a number of new types were being developed, including the RF7, which was an RF4 with the more powerful engine of the RF5; the RF5B Sperber, which was an RF5 of increased wing span and a modified cockpit canopy; the Sportavia S-5 and the RF6-180, which was still at the mock-up stage.

The second Sperber was experimentally fitted with a two cylinder 65hp Franklin engine, but this proved not to be a success due to high noise and vibration levels.

The Sportavia S-5 was a one-off quiet aircraft adaptation of the RF5 for the German Government. It used a Lycoming 115hp engine driving a three blade propeller. The exhaust was heavily silenced, being led into boxes on either side of the fuselage, where cooling air was also admitted. The exhaust finally exited aft of the rear cockpit. The prototype was under construction in the spring of 1971 and was flying by the summer. It was spookily quiet. One would hear an engine noise, suggestive of a VW Beetle about a mile away and then look up and find the S-5 almost directly overhead. Noise measurements revealed that, at the same distance, the S-5 was quieter than a K-7 glider with its airbrakes out.

One evening, we experienced an unforgettable and somewhat shocking experience. We two were walking with three girls, including Birgit and Michaela, back from the sports ground, where there had been some sort of a party.

It was approaching 11pm and the back road that we were on was lit only by the moonlight. As we walked down the lane past a small building on the right, I happened to look back over my shoulder to realise that we had just walked past a body lying at the side of the road. There was a stream of blood running down the road surface, in the moonlight, a sight of almost grotesque horror.

We all yelled and ran a few yards down the lane before stopping to decide what to do next. The girls were understandably upset and didn't want to stay there by themselves. We sent Birgit and Michaela to the nearest house to call for a doctor and the police. Jim stood down the lane with the third girl in case someone else came along and wanted to know what was happening.

Our limited German would not have coped with that situation. I went back to the body and realised that the young man concerned had attempted to kill himself by cutting his wrists. There were a number of razor blades lying around, which I carefully started to pick up. Shortly thereafter, he started to recover consciousness and to look for the razor blades so that he could try again. Fortunately, just about then, the girls returned with numerous people, the police and a doctor.

Whilst this was a thoroughly scary and frightening event, it was seen to be a good effort on our part by the village in general and Birgit and Michaela's parents in particular. We eventually left Schmidtheim by train en route to Skopje, Macedonia, leaving behind unforgettable memories, having had an enormously enjoyable time, and learned that if you are prepared to muck in, you can have a great time, even in a country where you can't speak the language.

Above: The prototype RF5B Sperber ballasted for aft cg trials

Below: The prototype RF7 D-EHAP masked-up in preparation for application of its registration

The one-off experimental Sportavia S5 Quiet Aircraft

BADGE NO: 165

MEDIA
APRIL 21, 1990

NAME: Jim Smith

AFFILIATION: British Embassy

Jim Smith

Chapter Seventeen

"We can't invite you as an honoured guest but you can come as part of the media"

When you work in the British Embassy and have many colleagues in the Royal Air Force, surprising opportunities arise; in this case, Jim being accredited as a member of the media to witness the first public showing of the F-117 stealth fighter at Nellis Air Force Base.

In November 1988, the first grainy pictures of the 'Stealth Fighter' or F-117A were released by the USAF. Rumours and disinformation about stealth aircraft had been appearing by then since about 1980, but their existence was consistently denied by the authorities.

The fuzzy photos showed an aircraft of a very unusual shape, but no real detail could be discerned. By the time the aircraft was acknowledged to exist, it had, in fact, been fully operational for 5 years. Two 'Have Blue' demonstrators flew in 1977, followed by the first production aircraft in June 1981. In early 1990, increasing detail on the aircraft was becoming available. The operational squadron was based at Tonopah, New Mexico, where operations had been conducted under strict security conditions. By 1990, the USAF wanted to move to a more conventional mode of operations, to move the aircraft to a more convenient base and to operate the aircraft in conjunction with other assets.

At that time, I was working in a scientific liaison role in the Air Force Staff attached to the British Embassy in Washington DC. I became aware that the US Air Force was planning to reveal the aircraft to the media, VIP guests, and families of the aircrew.

Clearly this event would be of great technical interest, and since my responsibilities covered areas such as aerospace research, technology and technology demonstrators, I asked one of my senior Air Force colleagues to see if he could get me an invite to the event.

A phone call was duly made to Tactical Air Command, who after a lengthy pause (actually it was three days) came back with the answer quoted above.

I was aware that information about the aircraft was currently available to those few with a 'Need to Know', but also that the public unveiling of the aircraft would provide an opportunity to gather open source information and photos which could be released to UK researchers and Industry with an interest in aircraft design for low radar signature.

So, armed with a list of features of interest to photograph, some of which were a bit surprising, and carrying a badge identifying me as 'British Embassy – Media', I set off for Las Vegas and Nellis Air Force Base, where the event was to occur.

Ron writes about Las Vegas from the air in another of these articles; I have to say that from the ground, it was a startling place.

I suppose, given that Las Vegas has an international reputation for glamour and glitz as perhaps the premier gambling town in the USA, I should not have been surprised at the gambling machines in the baggage hall at the airport.

Nevertheless, I certainly was surprised to find gambling machines installed within the Men's restroom!

Basically, Las Vegas is a rather unappealing town, located in 'middle of nowhere' Nevada, and dressed up to the nines to attract the tourist and his gambling dollar.

Above: Tony Tolin taxies 'the black jet' towards the waiting families and visitors at Nellis AFB, Las Vegas NV
Below: The second aircraft, flown by Lt Col Ralph Getcell, on parade for the families and press

A striking pose for the aircraft and its armed guard

It looked magnificent at night, lit up with sparkling lights, laser shows down 'The Strip' (Main Street), and the fountain at the Mirage Hotel, which turned into a volcano every half hour, looking extremely spectacular. But, at least in 1990, it was a dusty, tawdry town in daylight hours.

But I wasn't there for the town. I was there to go to Nellis Air Force Base, home of the Red Flag air combat exercises, and the chosen site for the unveiling of the F-117.

At the air base, the arrangements were a little unusual. The media were located at a stand immediately to the side of the VIP area, with the families some distance away. I noticed the media were quite observant, and not a little puzzled by my badge. However, inquisitiveness about me was soon forgotten when at the appointed hour, two small specks appeared on the horizon, and rapidly resolved themselves to be like no aircraft we had seen before. The two aircraft swept overhead, joined the circuit and landed, streaming large black parachutes. They then taxied slowly into the viewing area and stopped in front of the VIP guests.

After a short pause while the aircraft were shut down, the pilots climbed out, and the aircraft canopies were secured, a perimeter was established around the aircraft, and the media were called forward. In fact, the media milled around the aircraft for at least half an hour, much to the annoyance of the VIPs and the Families. But I wasn't complaining, I had a perfect opportunity to photograph the aircraft in minute detail, and to savour the moment at which this extraordinary aircraft was unveiled to the public for the first time, eight years after its first flight.

As the photos show, the F-117 is an extraordinary aircraft in every way. Flat-bottomed and with a remarkable triangular fuselage, the aircraft really does look like something from the movie 'Star Wars'.

Close up, radar signature reducing measures like the grids over the engine intake; the gold coating to the canopy; the radar absorbing appliqué coating; with tape and even radar absorbing putty covering gaps around access panels and filling the holes in the fasteners become evident.

Following the photo opportunity, a Press Conference was held in the Red Flag briefing room. There were two great moments in the Conference, the first of which was in answer to a question asking the detachment commander, Tony Tolin, what his thoughts were as he taxied the aircraft out to take off for the very first time.

He replied "Well, you have to realise, not only is it a funny looking aircraft, it is a single-seater, with no training aircraft, and the cockpit layout is unusual because of the shape. And of course, it will be at night, pitch black, and with no moon, that's how we operate the aircraft. So when you turn onto the runway and line up to take off for the first time, what you are thinking is 'I hope it flies like the simulator'".

Quite clearly authentic – the only answer a pilot could give, given the nature of the aircraft.

The second such moment was the response to the following question "We've been hearing these rumours that you have an alien (in this context alien = American for foreign national) flying the aircraft, can you comment?"

To which the reply, said with a straight face, was "That's correct. We have an RAF Squadron Leader flying the aircraft. He's been with us for two years – it's a standard exchange posting". This was a jaw-dropping moment for the US media. An RAF pilot had been flying the aircraft operationally for 2 years before the media had seen the aircraft. In fact, the first RAF pilots had flown the aircraft in 1985, two pilots making 5 flights each. This was one of those rare moments when the 'special' end of the 'special relationship' between the UK and the USA was made visible. The pilot in question was later a close colleague of mine. He was the project pilot on the Eurofighter project at a time when I was providing advice to that project on weight, aerodynamics and performance. Sadly, he was later to die in a flying accident in 1999. Vale Graham Wardell, first RAF exchange pilot of the F-117.

From head-on – a pyramid with wings; a science
fiction aircraft if ever there was one

Jim Smith

Chapter Eighteen
"Flightpath Revision"

A University Aeronautical Engineering degree course sometimes seems a bit far removed from the aircraft themselves ...until it is time for revision

One of the great pleasures of student life, compared to that at boarding school, was the freedom of action resulting from the ability to take responsibility for how time was used. As students in the Engineering Faculty, we had a much more demanding lecture programme than many, but nevertheless the days were far less scripted than at boarding school.

This meant that it was possible to follow a range of interests alongside the lecture program; with our continuing interest in aviation we were able to visit local airfields and, in particular, spend time down at Eastleigh A irport, which was an easy cycle ride from the University Halls of Residence complex at Swaythling. For transport, we cycled everywhere, owning a series of second-hand bikes. This was the inevitable result of an endemic problem of bicycle theft in Southampton at the time. Even with a good lock, it was relatively rare to be able to keep possession of a bicycle for more than six months before some lout would steal it, starting the search for yet another bargain bike.

It was not long before we discovered a path across some open ground leading up from close to The White Swan public house to the end of the runway at the airport. At weekends, in gaps in the lecture timetable, and particularly in the periods set aside for revision ahead of annual examinations, we could be found laying on the grass, reading lecture notes or text books (or just sunbathing) waiting for aircraft to pass overhead on their way to land.

The airport of those days was a relatively quiet location. While there were regular flights coming and going to the Channel Islands and to London, it could not be said to be a busy airport.

The regular visitors were British Island Airways flights, generally using Handley Page Heralds, but occasionally a Dakota; British European Airways Vickers Viscounts, Aurigny Airlines Britten -Norman Islander, Trislanders and Caledonian BAC One Elevens.

An Avro XIX of Thruxton-based Kemp's Aerial Surveys

Bristol Freighter

The airfield was also regularly visited by the Beech Barons and Piper Cherokees used for training professional pilots at the College of Air Training at Hamble.

However, these regulars were interspersed with light aircraft, many of them foreign registered, and with occasional charters and freight aircraft, including Aviation Traders Carvairs of British Air Ferries; the Aer Turas Bristol Freighter; Intra Airlines DC-3; and the Avro Ansons of Kemp's Aerial Surveys, usually based at Thruxton.

The actual location for this studious activity was adjacent to the last and lowest approach light, very close to the end of the runway and now buried under the M27 Motorway. At this spot, the passing aircraft were really quite low. We share an abiding memory of the whooshing sound of the wing tip vortices, particularly from the heavier aircraft, as they drifted across after the aircraft had passed, rustling leaves and ruffling the pages of one's textbook. Of course, as well as actually studying, a variety of other activities could be conducted.

For example, with practice, enthusiasm, and a fixed-wheel bicycle, the art of performing a 180 degree skid turn on a bicycle could be perfected, accompanied by a pleasingly impressive shower of gravel and dust. Other activities included using the remarkably friendly 'fruit machine' or 'one-armed bandit' at the White Swan (or more correctly, The Mucky Duck, as it was universally known). This machine was so friendly that we would generally arrive, play the machine and use the winnings to buy lunch.

On another occasion we carried out an entertaining but fruitless search to see if we could find any remains from the Cierva Air Horse, an extraordinary triple-rotor helicopter that had crashed in the area some 20 years previously. Sqn Ldr HA 'Alan' Marsh was the Chief Test Pilot of the Cierva Autogiro Co Ltd and a highly experienced rotary wing pilot.

He and his flight crew lost their lives following a fatigue failure of one of the Air Horse rotor heads. At the time, Ron had not the slightest notion that, as a promising young helicopter engineer, he would subsequently receive the Royal Aeronautical Society's Alan Marsh Award, gaining five hours of helicopter flying instruction as a result.

Whilst we were unsuccessful in our search, we did gain some insights into why it might be practically impossible to locate any evidence. The ground near the River Itchen was so poorly drained that apparently firm ground could in some areas actually be floating vegetation. Instead of the usually ankle-deep mud of this normally soft ground, some of the 'mud' in this area was at least waist deep. It was immediately clear that if there was anything to be found, it would certainly be buried under many feet of almost liquid mud. Once experienced, never forgotten!

Avro Anson

CITY OF CORK

AER TU

Aer Turas used a variety of aircraft for racehorse transport including this Bristol Freighter

Above: A DC3 providing INTRA Jersey's Channel Island service
Below: Kemps' Avro Ansons at their Thruxton base

Above: INTRA Douglas DC3
Below: An Air UK Herald on the Channel Islands run

Above: A rare visit from a British Air Ferries Carvair
Below: A BEA Viscount on another regular Channel Islands service

Above: An Aer Turas Douglas DC-4 in characteristic nose-down approach attitude
Below: A Cambrian BAC One Eleven at a late stage of its approach

A British United BAC One Eleven

Helen Tempest wing-walking at West Malling

Jim Smith

Chapter Nineteen

"Would you like to go to an airshow in a Chipmunk?"

A cautionary tale about the need to stay in practice, pay attention to the weather forecast and keep a good lookout, told against the backdrop of flying to an impressive airshow in Kent.

Well, there's only one answer to a question like that – "Of course I would, what's the deal?" – an answer that led to the two scariest moments I've experienced in flying to date.

The enquiry had come out of the blue, over the phone, from a lady pilot I had not met.

She explained that she had an invitation to bring 'Delta Delta', the Chipmunk belonging to the RAE Aero Club, over to the West Malling Air Show in Kent, the following weekend.

She was ringing me because she was not all that experienced in cross-country flying, and I had been recommended to her as someone who was likely to be keen to come, and who would be able to keep an eye on her navigation for her.

Of course, as it was her trip, all I had to do was come along for the ride.

Naturally, I was flattered, and equally naturally I said I would be happy to fly as her passenger and keep her on track. With hindsight, well, I suppose I could have asked her how many hours she had, and how many were tailwheel, and perhaps why the relatively short hop from Hampshire to Kent would be a challenge.

The day of the flight dawned bright and breezy – very breezy. The wind at the surface was 20 to 25kt from a westerly direction, which might make the aircraft a bit of a handful on the ground.

However, it was pretty much straight down the runway at Farnborough, and conveniently the runway at West Malling was aligned with that at Farnborough. At altitude, well, at 2000 ft, the wind would be stronger, perhaps 30 kt, and would be a direct tailwind. With a modest cruise speed of 90 kt, the Chippie would be blazing down the track to Kent at 120kt groundspeed.

We got the aircraft out, completed the checks, started up and taxied out, with myself in the back, feeling relaxed, and noting the care with which my lady pilot took the aircraft first downwind and then across the wind to the holding point in the brisk wind.

Line up on the runway, directly into wind, tail up with no noticeable swing, and we are airborne.

The climb out and turn downwind to set heading was routine, and off we went.

The navigation was simple, but had to be precise. Essentially straight down wind, passing to the north of Guildford and Dorking, and then along the motorway to the south of the high ground of the North Downs, the high point of which is about 900 ft above sea level.

Care was required not only because of the high ground, but because of the narrow gap between the London Heathrow Controlled Airspace to the north, and the London Gatwick Controlled Airspace to the south.

Shortly after we set course, I noticed my pilot was edging to the north.

After a few minutes, and a gentle reminder, we were abeam Dorking, and 3 miles north of track, getting very close to the London Control Zone.

After another reminder, and bearing in mind that I was there to look after the navigation "I have control" – a 15 degree heading change for 5 minutes or so brought us back on track.

I re-set the planned heading, checked that we were tracking to put the motorway on our left, to avoid danger of collision in the gap between the London and Gatwick Control Zones, and handed over to my pilot, explaining that all she needed to do was to hold the current heading.

She had mistaken Dorking for Guildford because of our high groundspeed, but had clearly not been able to detect that she was diverging from the track.

West Malling duly arrived on the nose; we made the necessary radio calls and joined downwind for runway 25. With the wind, although strong, only 5 deg off the runway direction, the approach was good and the touchdown was gentle.

I noted from the radio calls that a Harvard had been cleared to make a low pass over the runway, and just as I relaxed, the aircraft swung sharply left, and rolled on to the grass.

And then, just as I reached for the hand-operated brake, my lady pilot slammed the throttle wide open, and we had an exciting few moments.

We careered across the grass – a rather terse "I have control" from me.

Kick the aircraft straight, the tail is up, "Delta Delta is overshooting" on the radio, smartly followed by the Harvard calling that he was aborting his low pass, and we climb out.

A small voice from the front "Jim, can we go home now?" To which I respond "no, we're here now, let's enjoy the airshow".

As I climbed out and turned downwind, it dawned on me that I would now need to land the aircraft from the back seat for the first time, and in a relatively strong wind. Not too bad until you get into the flare – the nose comes up, the forward view disappears, and I land by looking out over the side, and observing the shadow of the aircraft nearing the runway.

Actually, it turned out to be a good landing, no issues at all. Taxy in, then park up the aircraft and report in. No mention of our gaffe on the first time around.

In the control tent, I spot Helen, an aerobatic enthusiast I knew who, it turned out, was now a wing walker with a Stearman display team. We passed a few moments reminiscing about the World Aerobatics Championship of 1986, where we had worked together judging the pilots' ability to stay in the competition box.

Duly checked in, we enjoyed the show.

At the time, the West Malling show was the premier warbird flying event in the UK.

As well as the magnificent Mustangs, Spitfires and the Battle of Britain Memorial flight, highlights of the show included a Thunderbolt; Kittyhawk; the only Skyraider display I have seen; some great mixed formations; a De Havilland Dragon display; and of course the Stearmans.

The RAE Aero Club Chipmunk G-BDDD, based at Farnborough

Above: The RAF Battle of Britain Memorial Flight
Below: A rare sight in Europe, a Vietnam-era Douglas Skyraider in the Kent skies

Above: The spectacular West Malling airshow featured many wartime aircraft. Here we see a Spitfire and a Chance Vought Corsair
Below: Mustang and P-40 in close formation

Above: A Magnificent fighter formation at West Malling – a Spitfire leads the top 5 US fighters of WW II. The aircraft are, clockwise from the top: Curtiss P-40 Kittyhawk; Chance-Vought Corsair; Supermarine Spitfire; Republic Thunderbolt; Grumman Bearcat; and North American Mustang. These six aircraft probably represent the finest allied fighter aircraft of the Second World War.

Below: Antonov An2 – probably the World's biggest single engine biplane

Above: Pre-war de Havilland DH84 Dragon preserved by Aer Lingus

Above Middle: The Grumman TBM3 Avenger   Below: Republic P-47 Thunderbolt

Helen spotted me as the aircraft taxied in after the display, and her greeting from on top of the top wing was so enthusiastic the commentator observed that she had clearly spotted an admirer in the crowd.

As the time to leave neared, it became clear that my pilot was becoming very nervous. I had indicated to her that she should fly back, because the practice would help.

The wind had dropped, although there were some heavy clouds about and I thought it unlikely that she would have much trouble with the landing.

It turned out that she knew the Commander Experimental Flying at Farnborough and that he was here in the Mustang G-SUSY.

She was very concerned not to have any more embarrassment in his presence and was much relieved, as we waited in the long queue for departure, to see the Mustang airborne ahead of us.

Eventually, we get away, climb out and set heading towards the West for the return trip. As we get close to the narrow passage between the two London Control Zones, I can see we are in for trouble. There is a large shower cloud, with heavy rain under it, right in the gap.

I quickly run through the options.

Divert to Biggin Hill – no, Biggin is on the high ground, and also under the heavy rain.

Divert to Redhill – it is also under the rain, but on lower ground, so might be a possibility.

But I have never flown there and am aware that there are special procedures as the airfield sits under the Gatwick Zone.

Return to West Malling – clearly the sensible option, but it was by now quite late, and a diversion to West Malling would leave us stuck for the night.

Moreover, both of us had changed into flying suits and neither had transferred either money or credit cards, so we would be really stuck.

Can we get through?

Looking at the cloud, I can see the orange glow from the sinking sun below the cloud. This tells me that the weather will be clear on the other side of the cloud.

With maybe 5 minutes flying just below the cloud, we should come out the other side into fair weather for the return to Farnborough.

As we approach the cloud, the rain becomes torrential. Understandably, my lady pilot handed control over to me.

I crept along, keeping clear of the high ground to my right, gradually being forced lower as we reached the heaviest cloud and rain. It was unbelievably noisy – my companion said later she was concerned the canopy would break.

Visibility was very poor.

I had no trouble flying the aircraft; I just concentrated on not entering cloud while staying as high as I could, maintaining a westerly heading and keeping away from the high ground.

After a very tense 5 minutes, we burst out into clear air. I handed over control, and we made our way back to Farnborough.

It was now about 8 pm, winds were light, and we joined the circuit.

Having called when the airfield was in sight, we knew that the tower was not manned.

As we turned finals, I suggested we make a courtesy radio call in case anyone was in the area.

"Delta Delta, finals to land, runway 25 Farnborough" was met, to my surprise with an immediate response

"Golf Sierra Yankee, Mustang, late downwind, Farnborough".

Immediately, realising this was the Commander Experimental Flying, my passenger panicked –"Jim, you have control, I need you to do the landing again".

At this point, with the aircraft on short finals, what else was I to do.

Another uneventful landing was achieved from the back seat.

We taxied in, closed down and got out of the aircraft, for an interesting de-brief.

My pilot was very relieved that we had got back safely, as was I.

However, for her own good, I had to tell her that she should not fly again until she had had a thorough check out from our Chief Flying Instructor, and that she should also do a practice cross-country with him as well.

So now the reader is wondering about the two scary moments.

Well the first was when my pilot, having swung off the runway, slammed open the throttle and we began careering across the grass.

The second – not the landing from the back; not even the noise and the sheer concentration on flying as we crept through the rain shower; and not the landing a Farnborough.

The second scary moment was the half-seen aircraft passing us in the opposite direction at the very worst point under the cloud.

At exactly the same height - constrained by the cloud and the visibility and within about 100 ft of being in exactly the same place - dictated by the high ground and controlled airspace.

Someone else had made essentially the same series of bad decisions as me, and somehow, we had both got away with it.

Delta Delta - a thoroughbred trainer with delightful handling characteristics

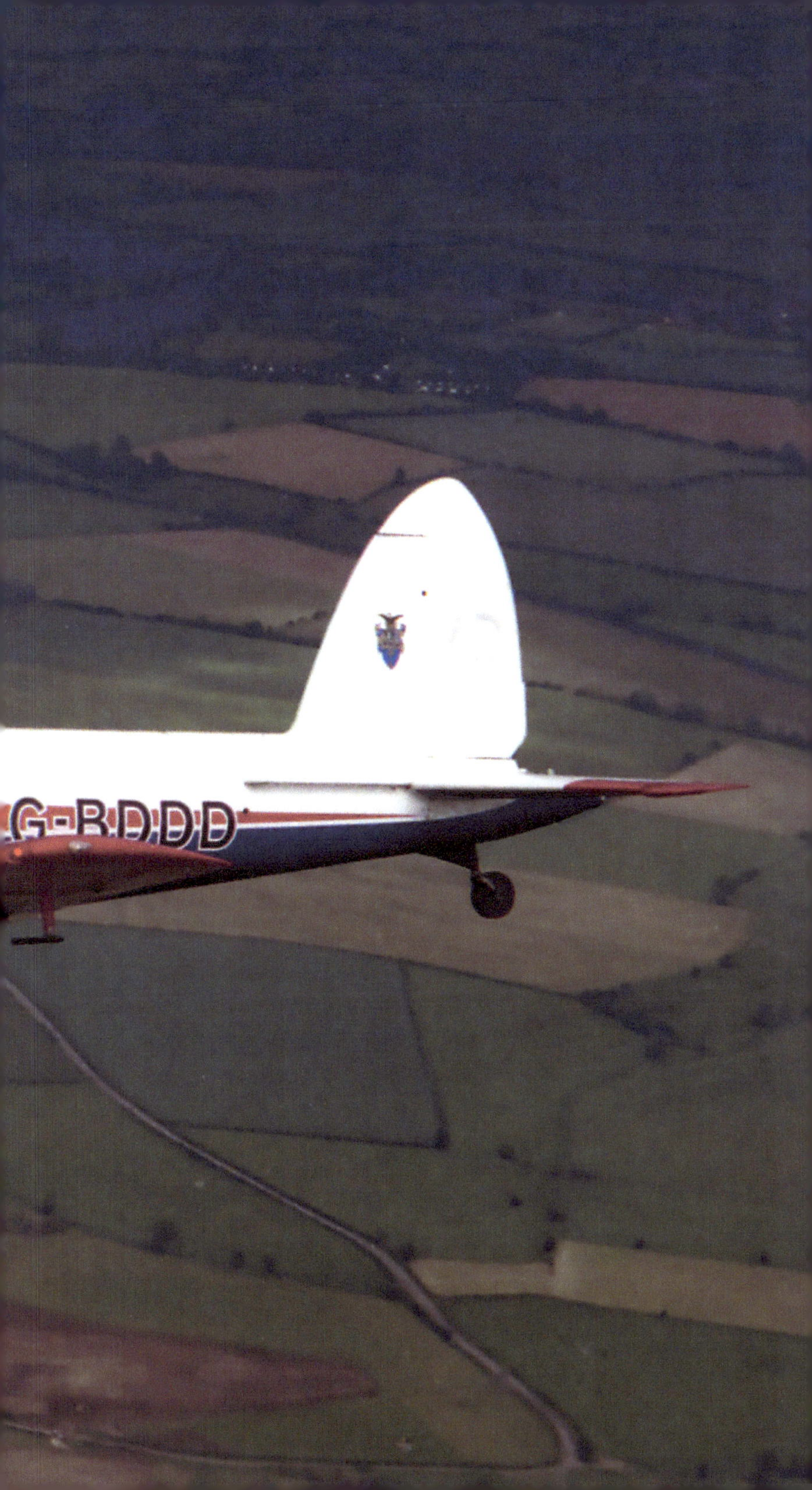
G-BDDD

Ron Smith

Chapter Twenty
"Throttle Set, Contact!"

Ah! De Havilland. The unforgettable experience of flying the Tiger Moth biplane from the beautiful hill top airfield of Compton Abbas.

As a preamble, I suppose that I should say that I am no great expert - I am not a test pilot, nor am I a well-known display pilot, or have any other great claim to fame in terms of piloting expertise.

I gained my PPL some 32 years ago, and have accumulated some 750 hours of experience, flying mainly tailwheel aircraft. I learned on Cessnas, but the first tailwheel type that I flew was the de Havilland DH82A Tiger Moth.

The Tiger Moth is an open cockpit biplane, with the crew sitting in tandem, with the pilot in the rear seat. The aircraft has no starter motor, no brakes and a tail skid.

The wings are fitted with Handley Page automatic slats to delay the stall, which rise, as if by magic, from the wing leading edge when the wing incidence increases beyond a particular point.

One enters the aircraft by stepping on the left wing root walkway and then across into the cockpit - usually stepping straight onto the seat. The aircraft was originally designed to be flown wearing a seat parachute pack.

Entry and exit can be an inelegant process

In civil use, with no parachute, there then follows a trial and error exercise with cushions to get sat at the right level, following which the harness can be done up. When I flew the aircraft, this was by means of a Sutton Harness, where a peg is inserted through a selected hole in each waist strap and shoulder strap, and then secured by a pin. One certainly feels fixed in place as a result. If you have short arms it is a good idea to switch on the fuel (a push-pull knob on the lower left side of the cockpit, but placed well forward) before doing up the straps and then finding that you can't reach the control knob! The cockpit is usually painted that unique military shade 'cockpit green' with a rich smell of fuel and oil. With no starter or brakes, the aircraft is started by swinging the propeller requiring skilled help and a ritual incantation between prop-swinger and pilot before the final 'throttle set' and 'contact!' after which the engine (hopefully) bursts into life. Safety is helped by the fact that the critical magneto switches are positioned outside the cockpit so that the prop-swinger can see for himself whether they are on or off.

After running up the engine and checking the magneto drops one taxies slowly to the take-off point. This requires care to weave the aircraft nose from side to side to avoid taxiing into unseen objects.

Also, as one is moving downwind and with no brakes, the speed must be kept low, particularly if the ground is also sloping. Having the aircraft roll quietly down a slope toward a fence with no brakes and no effective steering concentrates the mind!

On take-off, one completes the limited pre-take off checks, lines the aircraft up on the runway and, leaning to the side of the cockpit to improve forward view, picks a mark to help keep the aircraft straight. Full throttle is accompanied by a firm forward push on the stick to raise the tail. The aircraft wants to swing at this point due to gyroscopic and slipstream effects.

The amount of swing will depend on whether or not there is also a cross wind present, and on how fast the tail comes up.

Usually a fair amount of left rudder is required to keep straight, but once the tail comes up the aircraft accelerates quite quickly.

With the trim correctly set, the aircraft flies itself off the ground as take-off speed is reached.

On the aircraft that I flew, the advice when levelling out for the cruise was to throttle back until there was a marked reduction in noise level, and accept whatever speed resulted. This usually seemed to be around 85 knots.

Now there is time for first impressions. First, I can't really see very well where I am going - visibility in every other direction is spectacular.

The cockpit is draughty and, unless wearing very good windproof clothing, winter flights tend to be limited by the time taken for the pilot's hands and feet to lose all feeling.

For a novice pilot, the next challenge is maintaining balanced flight - the large Reid & Sigrist turn & slip indicator seems to have a life of its own. A feature that immediately becomes apparent is that there is a marked change in directional trim with every change in power (for most aircraft a change in pitch trim with power is more usual).

The result is that throttling back produces a brisk yaw to the left, and the novice is off chasing the turn & slip needles again. When I was just getting checked out on the type it took quite a while before I felt that I was in charge of the aeroplane, and not vice versa. Of course, once one has got it sorted out, there is also great satisfaction in then being able to carry out steep turn reversals with the slip needle bang in the centre throughout.

I found that landing was best accomplished from a glide approach. The aircraft nose is then well down, improving the forward view. If one is slightly high, a sideslip will simultaneously increase the rate of descent and improve the view still further. A long powered approach (perhaps due to following another aircraft) worsens the forward view and makes subsequent judgement of the landing more difficult.

A newly-restored Tiger Moth recaptures the spirit of the 1940s

My greatest difficulty was landing, like most Tiger Moth pilots. The undercarriage is good at softening the immediate landing impact, but has a tendency to throw one back into the air in a series of increasingly large, semi-ballistic bounces, if you get it wrong.

My eventual technique, which has stood me in good stead with many other tailwheel types, is as follows: *Glide toward the ground with the throttle fully closed and aim to level off with the wheels just above the ground. Once level, the aircraft will slow up quite quickly and start to settle. On feeling this, one progressively brings the stick right back and holds it there as the aircraft rotates to the landing attitude and touches down. The advantage here is that if one levels off slightly high, the aircraft, because it has already slowed down, will not have enough energy to initiate a series of kangaroo bounces at touch-down. After touch-down, and still with the stick right back and throttle closed, one tries to pick up any swing or change of direction as quickly as possible, immediately applying rudder to stop the swing. This is a necessary technique on any tailwheel aircraft. The skill, like that of riding a bicycle, can only be acquired through experience, rather than following a step by step recipe. Provided the slip needle is centred, the stall is quite docile and the Handley Page slats minimise any tendency to a wing drop. If, however, the aircraft is stalled with any slip present, it immediately drops into a spin. The spin features a fairly high rate of rotation, and a steeply nose down attitude - this is quite exciting and not a little off-putting! Recovery is straightforward following application of full opposite rudder and forward stick.*

In summary, the Tiger Moth is a training aircraft that requires good skill levels to fly consistently well. It is rewarding to fly well and delightful to watch. I am very pleased to have learned my tailwheel flying on such a classic and the sights, sounds and smells of doing so have given me lasting pleasure.

Above: Taxying requires considerable care
Below: Ah! ... de Havilland. The DH Moth Club Rally at Woburn Abbey

VH-FXY at Moorabbin, showing its superb condition and extensive cockpit glazing

Ron Smith

Chapter Twenty-One
"To Point Cook via Vietnam"

All observation aircraft require great visibility for the crew and excellent handling. This was much in evidence when Ron accepted an invitation to fly with magazine   editor Rob Fox in his immaculately restored ex-Vietnamese Cessna Birddog from Melbourne to the RAAF Museum at Point Cook.

At the end of October 2006, I was visiting Australia on business and took the opportunity of following up an earlier invitation to catch up with Rob Fox (if I was back in Melbourne) and to go for a flight in his Cessna O-1G Birddog VH-FXY.

Rob is an aviation photographer and editor of Flightpath magazine. He had kindly reviewed my book series and we had stayed in contact as a result.

Sunday 29th October saw my twin brother Jim and I at Moorabbin Airport, helping Rob open up his hangar, which contained a truly enticing group of aeroplanes. There was a Europa, the late Clive Canning's Thorp T18 VH-CMC, which flew from Australia to Sywell in 1976, a Boeing Stearman, North American T-28 Trojan VH-CIA, a T-6 Harvard VH-TXN and Rob's Birddog, resplendent in its authentic South Vietnamese Air Force colour scheme.

After admiring the condition (immaculate) of the Birddog, Rob gave a quick run down on its restoration which included the repair of numerous bullet holes in the fuselage, complete replacement of the cockpit floor and the re-skinning of the entire wing. The aircraft has many original features, including its original smoke marker launcher tubes, hanging on their sway-braces beneath the wings.

With the aircraft outside, Rob suggested that he fly me over to the RAAF Museum at the Point Cook base (established 1914), whilst Jim drove over there (a forty minute drive, or so). Once Jim arrived, Rob would also give him a quick circuit, before getting on with the other business of the day.

I installed myself in the rear seat – the Birddog is a tandem two-seater equipped with (whisper it......) real sticks – not the plastic push pull yokes normally associated with the Cessna breed. The lap strap had the same fastening as my own Luscombe 8A, and the shoulder harness was fitted with inertia reels.

Parked outside the RAAF Museum office at Point Cook

Rob fitted the rear stick (which was clipped into a housing on the port side of the rear cockpit wall when not in use) and pointed out the rudder pedals that were stowed flat on the rear cockpit floor, but could be flicked up in flight if required.

With a loud noise from the electric pump, Rob squirted fuel into the engine and turned the starter, the engine responding immediately.

As we moved off, I was immediately struck by the smooth undercarriage, the very smooth running of the engine and the excellent all round view afforded by the extensive cockpit glazing.

We lined up for take-off with about 15 degrees of flap set and the aircraft surged forward as Rob opened the throttle, becoming airborne in about 7 seconds and climbing out with a very steep gradient. We climbed out to 2,000 feet before levelling off, looking out for a Robinson R44 that passed between us and the city and a Cessna 172 that passed between us and the coast, both inbound to Moorabbin.

As we approached the coast to the south of the city Rob invited me to fly the aeroplane. "Not above 2,500. Fly along the coast for a mile or so and then head out across the bay. Once over the bay you can play with the aircraft for a bit before we head for Point Cook". Rob moved slightly to his right so that I could see the altimeter and airspeed indicator.

After asking for a small trim adjustment, I felt the controls and found sensitive elevators, and effective rudder and slightly heavy ailerons, albeit with much less aileron drag than my Luscombe.

Over Phillip Bay I completed a gentle turn left and right before steep turning in each direction with the internal cockpit diagonal struts tracking round the horizon. The aircraft gave an immense feeling of confidence, due in part to the excellent all round view, the smooth engine and the effective controls. I was very pleased with my height keeping in the steep turns and the left to right roll during the turn reversal felt well balanced, although I couldn't see the slip ball to confirm this.

Rob Fox taxies out the Birddog to give Jim a ride
around the Point Cook circuit

Seeing Point Cook ahead, I headed for the airfield and Rob asked me to descend whilst aiming to fly across the centre of the airfield. A number of aircraft were flying left hand circuits on 17 hard and we were to position downwind right hand for 17 grass. After crossing the airfield I descended to circuit height and at Rob's prompting put down about half flap at the end of the downwind leg. I then turned base leg, throttling back to initiate a descent, turning finals fairly briskly to avoid conflicting with the final approach for the parallel hard runway.

Shortly after establishing on finals, Rob asked for more flap (full flap is 60 degrees and rarely used) and I asked him if the approach speed was OK. We had not discussed this before take-off and I was flying the aircraft by feel. 60 kts felt right and Rob seemed quite happy.

It was very noticeable (again unlike other Cessnas I have flown) that we had not needed to re-trim as increasing amounts of flap had been selected.

Rob had commented that I would notice this, provided one flew with the correct combinations of airspeed, flap and power settings. As I didn't experience it, I can't comment on whether there is a significant nose-up trim change on go-around with full flap and full power, which is certainly a feature of the Cessna 150 and 172.

On very late finals, Rob said "OK, I'll take it from here" and we landed, turned right and taxied across the grass in-field to park immediately outside the RAAF Museum flight office.

The Museum was closed due to a failure of the water supply, which meant that there were no toilet facilities. Jim and I had a quick tour of the flight/restoration hangar in compensation, with its on-going Mosquito restoration, Tiger Moth, Winjeel, Sopwith Pup replica and Commonwealth Mustang.

Jim had a trip round the circuit in the Birddog and after saying a big thank you to Rob for his generosity in flying us in his immaculate aircraft, we headed back to Melbourne.

Ron Smith

Chapter Twenty-Two

"Well you've got your slow landings sorted out"

Piper's classic Cub trainer in the Florida sunshine

Some years ago, I found myself travelling frequently to the US on business, either to Orlando, or to Arlington, Texas (midway between Dallas and Fort Worth). As the trips were often for ten days or more, I managed to squeeze in some flying in both locations.

This is a little tale of my experiences flying a Cub in Florida.

I drove north from Orlando out past Apopka and found myself driving next to a light aviation field called Orlando Country Airport (now known as Orlando Apopka Airport).

I pulled in and soon found myself having coffee with the two ladies who ran the place.

Country charm personified, they answered my question of whether there were any tail wheel aeroplanes available to hire with the response "Have you seen our runway?" from one of them, and "Would you like to buy a tee shirt?" from the other.

The tee shirt said "I survived the cross-winds at Orlando Country Airport".

The runway was a concrete strip, just 28ft wide running at 45 degrees to the prevailing Floridian wind – no, there were no tail wheel aircraft for hire, or even based there!

They told me to continue down the road and turn left at the intersection with the orange flashing light (Jones Avenue) and look out for signs to an airstrip on my right. This turned out to be Bob White Field (now known as Potter Airport). It had a single east-west grass strip and four hangar blocks full of interesting aircraft, with a notably high proportion of Stearman biplanes.

On asking, I was told that Tim Preston would rent out tailwheel aircraft.

When I eventually caught up with him, he said that he had an Aeronca O-58A, a J-3 Cub and a Stearman.

The Stearman he would instruct in, dual only, for $100 an hour, and as far as the other two were concerned, "If you show me you can fly them, then you can fly them". He also explained that most of his tail wheel checkouts were either "for airline pilots who've decided it's time to buy a Stearman" or for FAA examiners, who've never flown a tailwheel aircraft and "need to check out airline pilots in Stearmans".

Classic Yellow Piper J-3 Cub in the Florida sun

The Stearmans were being rebuilt to a fantastically high standard on a private strip at Zelwood, a couple of miles away.

I got checked out in the Aeronca O-58 and the Cub and also had an hour of crosswind landings in the Stearman. I flew the Aeronca to a nearby airfield at Eustis (now known as the Mid Florida Air Service Airport) and had a bit of trouble getting it started again – Tim preferred one to swing the O-58 prop whilst standing behind it (so that you could reach the throttle inside the cockpit), which I found distinctly uncomfortable.

When I first flew the Cub, he sat me in the back (normally this is the solo pilot position, or the instructor position for dual training), saying that as most people he taught wanted to fly Stearmans, it was best they got used to a lousy forward view from the outset. After we'd been flying for a few minutes, Tim said "You're doing fine, I'm happy with the flying, but you are tense on the controls and I'm waiting for you to relax". This was fair comment; as the fine Florida weather was setting off multiple thermals and the Cub was getting bounced around.

I quite like the Cub and, at least in Floridian conditions, it's great to fly along with the door open and the window up and a big empty space in next to you. I've flown 65, 90, 105 and 150 hp Cubs and have always found precise trimming difficult (they use a handle on the sidewall of the cockpit to change the angle of incidence of the fixed part of the tailplane to change trim).

The other notable feature in Florida was that there was almost always water in the fuel due to the enormously fluctuating temperature and humidity – Tim was completely unfazed when I first pointed it out. He just said "That's why we check it before every flight".

Tim duly sent me off by myself;

I said that I would fly around Lake Apopka and then "fly round the pattern a few times when I get back".

He said two things in response. The first was "Watch out for the TV masts".

Above: The warm and sunny conditions are ideal for flying the Cub with the window open
Below: I finished my hour's flying in Tim's docile Stearman with one of my best ever landings

Above: Florida – flat, fine weather and full of alligator-infested lakes

Florida is so low and flat that the Apopka TV masts were about five times higher than the highest piece of terrain in Florida, which is 'Mount' Dora at all of 300 feet. He also said "Make sure that you flare properly and get the stick right back on landing; if you do a little hop on the roll out, I'll know that you landed too fast." After I landed, I taxied over to the aircraft's bay in the open hangar structure and started to put it away.

As I did so, Tim came over and said "Well, you've got your slow landings sorted out". We walked together back across the runway and met the field owner Bob White on the other side.

He looked at me and said "Son, that was a sloooow landing. Hell, it was so slow, that if you hadn't liked it, you could have got out and walked!" I walked off, laughing, with some happy memories of Cub flying in Florida.

On a subsequent trip, I took a work colleague, Gary, flying in the Cub for a couple of sorties. Afterwards, we had a late lunch in Mount Dora, which we had been recommended to as the sort of place the locals go to for relaxation (and to avoid the tourists). Whilst we had been flying, I had explained to Gary that one did not fly over the many lakes in the area because of the alligators. I had learnt this after being given a ride in a locally-based Luscombe and being told off for cutting across the corner of Lake Apopka. The pilot then proceeded to drop to a lower height and fly round the lake spotting and pointing out numerous 'gators – quite a salutary experience. After lunch, we were sat by a small lake in Mount Zion watching people sailing and looking at the ospreys flying overhead. Gary said "Do you really think that there are alligators in this lake?"

I replied "Well, there are plenty of people sailing, but I can't see any swimming and, if you look to your right, there's a baby alligator on the bank. Where there are small ones, there are also big ones!"

Gary later sent a postcard to the office saying that 'It was an absolute privilege to fly with Ron, in such an old aeroplane …over alligator infested swamps!'

Ron Smith

Chapter Twenty-Three
"We've had a Telex about you!"

Alaska is 'America's Last frontier'. It's not hard to see why in this aeronautical tour (business trip) around Anchorage, Lake Hood, Merrill Field and their environs.

During my time as Head of Future Projects at Westland, I was involved in a number of collaborative programmes. One of these was known by the acronym GARTEUR, standing for Group for Aeronautical Research and Technology in Europe.

This sponsored joint Industry and Government research between European nations in areas that were not considered commercially sensitive.

In this instance through 1984 and 1985, we had been looking jointly at the market prospects for a high speed commercial rotorcraft like a compound helicopter (with auxiliary lift and propulsion), or a tilt rotor design.

A questionnaire was developed and a market survey was conducted visiting major commercial, military and paramilitary helicopter operators in the United States and Canada.

Each team comprised two individuals, one from the industry of one nation, teamed with a government representative from a different nation.

I was deputed to travel with a representative of the French Embassy in Washington DC, discussing our questionnaire with the US Army in the Pentagon; the US Coastguard at Fort Meade between Washington and Baltimore; Airspur, a commercial operator using the WG30 in Los Angeles; Okanagan Helicopters in Vancouver; Columbia Helicopters in Aurora, Oregon; Evergreen Helicopters at McMinnville, also in Oregon; and finally ERA Helicopters of Anchorage, Alaska.

Apart from the exciting itinerary, the next good news was that my French colleague was a gastronome and permanently in search of the best restaurant in any town or city we visited. He was also an expert in travelling around the US airline system making unlikely connections to minimise travel time.

We had had a number of very successful visits and had arrived in Oregon to see Columbia Helicopters. They could not have been more helpful.

After our discussions, they asked who we were seeing next and, on being told Evergreen in McMinnville, they explained that it was only just over twenty miles away and gave us detailed directions for the drive on the back-country roads of Oregon.

This was a huge benefit because, as a direct result, we were able to see Evergreen on the same day, whereas we had originally planned a day for each company.

At McMinnville we were also asked "Where are you going next?" to which we said ERA at Anchorage, explaining also that we had made up a day on our schedule and didn't know whether to spend it in Oregon or Alaska.

"Have you been to Alaska before?" No we had not. "You have to see Alaska, provided that the weather is going to be good. Why don't you phone up air traffic control at Anchorage International Airport and ask them what they expect tomorrow's local weather will be like?"

This was, self-evidently, an excellent suggestion, which we put into immediate effect.

Alaska is a land of survivors; this is an apparently airworthy Vertol H-44 Shawnee at Merrill Field

The weather was expected to be equally excellent, so we headed down to Portland and hopped on a plane to Anchorage.

On arrival, we had some difficulty finding a hotel room and eventually found rooms in a very basic establishment. Next day, we agreed that we would do some aviation exploring, seek out some glacier views and head north from Anchorage toward the Denali National Park, in the general direction of Mount McKinley.

Whilst Anchorage is not the most attractive town, it is a haven for all sorts of aircraft, many of them old and unusual. Not for nothing is Alaska known as 'America's Last Frontier'. The road north from Anchorage runs to Fairbanks in central Alaska.

From there, the famous 'Ice Road' or Dalton Highway continues north to Deadhorse and Prudhoe Bay on the Arctic Ocean. The region to the west of the Anchorage to Fairbanks road and the Dalton Highway is an area the size of France, with no roads at all. Outlying communities can be reached by ship, but most settlements are supplied by air cargo flights. There were a number of Boeing 747 cargo aircraft at the airport with a most extraordinary range of propeller driven cargo aircraft to provide onward distribution to smaller settlements.

The other immediately evident feature of life on the Last Frontier was that Anchorage must have the largest number of airfields in relation to its size than any other American city.

As well as the International Airport, there was Elmendorf Air Force Base, Lake Hood, Lake Hood Airstrip and Merrill Field. Lake Hood has been 'constructed' by joining two adjacent lakes (Lakes Hood and Spenard) together by a pair of canals, which act as the runways for a fantastically active seaplane base.

There are more than 700 aircraft based at Lake Hood. Lake Hood Airstrip is a gravel runway next to the lake, which is mainly used as the seasons change and the lake itself cannot reliably be used on either floats or skis.

Above: Some survivals from the days of early Alaskan aviation are preserved at the Pioneer Air Museum north of Anchorage
Below: Cargo aircraft of all sorts fly freight to out-lying communities; this is a Douglas C-133 Cargomaster

Above: A surviving Aviation Traders Carvair is an unexpected sight among the many cargo aircraft at Anchorage International Airport
Below: One of a number of Fairchild C-119s on the Anchorage ramp

Merrill Field is a tourist attraction in its own right; there were leaflets in the hotel saying "Come and see the bushplanes at Merrill Field".

There are around one thousand aircraft at Merrill Field, almost all of them of tailwheel configuration, often sporting extreme modifications that would never have entered into the head of their original designers.

Inland from Anchorage, we also found a small aviation museum with a number of relics of the real pioneering days of Alaskan aviation.

As promised, the weather was very good, as it remained the next day for our meeting at ERA Helicopters on the south side of the main airport.

From their offices, one could make out a distant snow-capped peak, appearing to hover in the sky on the northern horizon.

"Is that Mount McKinley?" I asked.

"Yes, it sure is."

"How far away is it?"

The answer was "Oh, about 140 miles".

Now that is unlimited visibility!

After two fascinating days in Anchorage, I headed for the airport for my return flight, which was leaving at midday on the Saturday.

When I went to check in, there was a huddled conversation behind the desk and I was told "Oh, Mr Smith, we've had a telex about you. The bad news is that there are no Business Class seats. … The good news is that you'll be going back First Class!"

The flight duly took off at midday and landed at Heathrow at around 06:30 on the Sunday morning.

A slightly confusing feature of the trans-polar route flown was that the entire flight from start to finish was conducted in broad daylight.

Above: The surviving Boeing YL-15 on the fringes of Lake Hood
Below: A de Havilland Beaver takes off from Lake Hood floatplane workhorse of the northern skies

Above: Piper Super Cub on truck wheels and tundra tyres at Lake Hood airstrip
Below: Another rare bird at Merrill Field a civilianised Convair L-13

Above: Republic Seabee at Lake Hood airstrip
Below: A Fairchild C-82 parked in front of its later development, the C-119 Packet , at Anchorage International

Above: One of the oldest cargo aircraft at Anchorage was this Curtis C-46 Commando. Its colour scheme suggests that it was previously in Japanese Self Defence Force service.   Below: Reeve Aleutian is a long-standing Alaskan airline. At this time it was operating the L188 Electra on passenger routes

Above: Another unusual aircraft of the Reeve Aleutian fleet is this NAMC YS-11 of Japanese origin
Below: The preserved remains of a Bellanca Pacemaker from the pioneering days

Above: A pre-war Curtis Robin sits on floats alongside Lake Hood
Below: Floatplanes can be seen on nearly every Alaskan lake. This is an Aeronca Sedan

This Grumman Goose sits, awaiting restoration, alongside Lake Hood

Ron Smith

Chapter Twenty-Four
"Halos and Hoodlums"

Russia was pretty much a closed book for a defence industry analyst during the Cold War. This visit to Moscow and Warsaw in 1992 provided a close look at the Russian and Polish helicopter industry and their supporting research and manufacturing facilities. This was not always a comfortable trip, but permission for photography was granted for most of the visit, resulting in some unique images.

It is 1992, and I was working in the Helicopter Engineering Department of British Aerospace, based in the old Sopwith and Hawker factory. The company is establishing the capability to act as Design Authority for the design, development, flight test and armament clearance of helicopters, whilst it competes for potential UK MoD helicopter procurements.

At the time of this visit, I had been encouraged to retain a high profile in the industry by continuing my activities with the Royal Aeronautical Society, as Chairman of the Rotorcraft Committee, and with the American Helicopter Society, where I was a member of the Technical Council.

With this background, I somewhat diffidently suggested to the management that I should like to go on a visit that was being planned to visit helicopter design, research, testing and production facilities in Russia and Poland.

To my surprise, the answer was yes, go by all means and write it up when you get back.

Now, the Berlin Wall had fallen as recently as November 1989, up to which point, the facilities that we proposed to visit had been of great interest in the context of understanding Soviet capabilities during the Cold War. Barely two-and-a-half years later, the opportunity was there to visit the Mil and Kamov design bureaux and their test facilities; the Central Aerohydrodynamics Institute (Russian abbreviation TsAGI) at Zhukovsky near Moscow; manufacturing facilities for the Mil Mi-26 Halo at Rostov on Don; and the PZL design and manufacturing centre at Lublin, Poland.

The trip was organised by People to People International and began with a flight from New York to Moscow via Amsterdam, on 12-13 June. The party was made up of a mix of retired personnel from US manufacturers; together with serving representatives from the US Army and Navy; myself; a lady from a private company that seemed to be a Washington Defense Consultant (or 'Beltway-bandit'); and a highly-knowledgeable helicopter historian and enthusiast from Switzerland, Peter Wernli.

Peter was a key member of the party, in that he was determined to photograph everything in sight. Although this caused a certain *frisson* among our hosts, permission was granted, everywhere except within TsAGI.

It was with some nervousness that we gave up our passports and sat waiting in the 'VIP' arrivals area at Moscow airport. Eventually, with no obvious immigration or customs procedure, we were ushered outside to a bus and told that all our baggage had already been loaded onto it – and so it proved.

Throughout the visit the party was given access to very senior individuals in the Russian industry; for example, the visits to Mil and TsAGI in Moscow and to the factory at Rostov were accompanied by Gurgen Karapetian, the Chief Test Pilot of the Mil Bureau.

The giant and ungainly Mil Mi-24 in storage

At the Mil Design Bureau, we had discussions with the General Designer, Mark Vineberg; the Chief Test Pilot; and Mr Samusenko, who was the project designer of the Mil Mi-26 Halo.

Within the Russian system, the Design Bureau is responsible for design, development, prototype manufacture and qualification of the design as ready for production. Production is then carried out in a manufacturing facility, which, given the geographical extent of the Soviet Union, could be remote from the Design Bureau.

From the design offices, the party were taken to the prototype development facility at Tomilino where the hangar contained a pair of Mi-26 Halos, an Mi-24 Hind and an Mi-34. There were a number of trials aircraft and discarded prototypes around the site, notably including a decommissioned example of the enormous Mil Mi-12. There was a treasure trove here including three Mi-28 Havocs, a discarded fenestron test article; a least eight Mi-24 and a similar number of Mi-26 Halo. There were three stored Mi-24 airframes, which appeared to cover the evolution of the design from the Hind A version through to the Hind D. A selection of additional photographs from this visit is presented in the gallery at the end of this piece. At the Kamov offices at Lyubertsy, the party was hosted by the General Designer Sergey Mikheyev, who stated that this was the first ever international visit to the Kamov Bureau. The products of the company and future developments were presented, from the hugely successful Ka-26 Hoodlum agricultural helicopter and its single and twin-turbine derivatives, the Ka-126 and Ka-226. The company was then actively working on the civil Ka-62 project, the Ka-50 co-axial attack helicopter, and the Ka-27 / Ka-32 Helix, which was a successor to the successful Ka-25 Hormone naval ASW helicopter. After introducing these current projects there was a lively discussion of past projects, based on a series of fascinating models on display in a cabinet at the end of the meeting room.

Above: A fearsome-looking Hind-D in the Mil experimental hangar
Below: Mil Mi-24 development aircraft at Tomilino

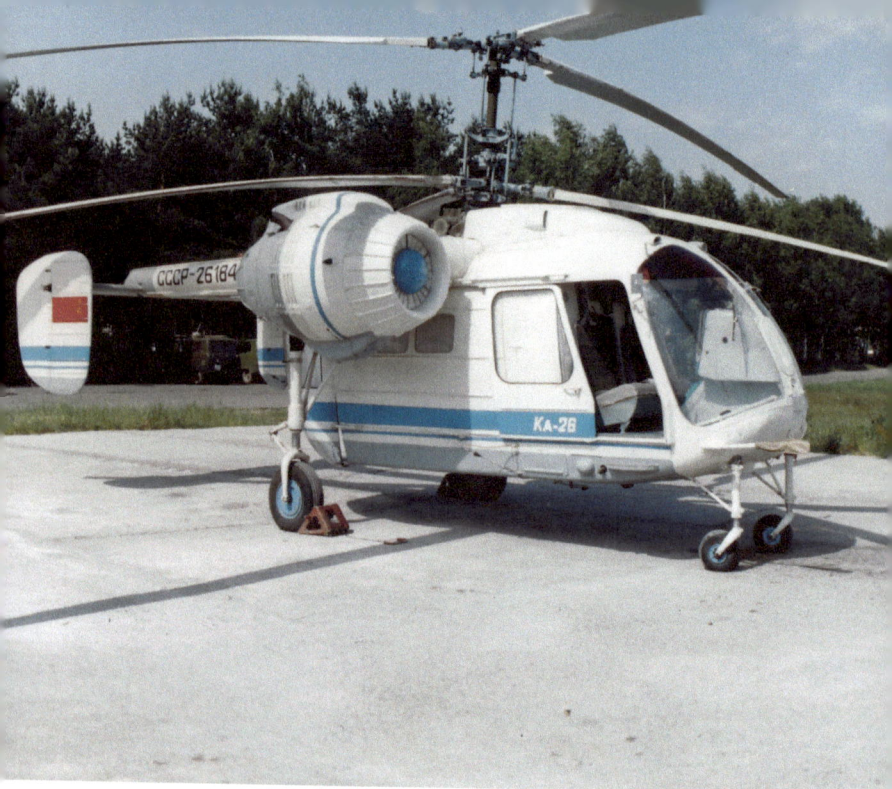

Above: The insect-like Ka-26 Hoodlum
Below: The sprightly Ka-27 Helix shipboard anti-submarine helicopter

From the offices, the party were taken to the nearby flight test facility, where examples of the Ka-26, Ka-126 and a pair of Ka-27 were available for inspection. One of the Ka-27 gave an extremely spirited flying display, being surprisingly quiet and highly manoeuvrable.

From Lyubertsy, the next visit was to the extraordinary test facilities at TsAGI at Zhukovsky. No photography was permitted here, but the visit revealed test installations, including multiple wind tunnel and structural test facilities, apparently constructed to meet every possible application. Until two years previously, the facility had been completely closed to foreigners, although I now understand that both Airbus and Boeing have offices locally.

There are more than 50 wind tunnels on the site and some phenomenal environmental test facilities developed to support the Soviet space programme. One of the impressive list of wind tunnels is T-128, a tunnel with a 2.75m square cross section that operates up to a Mach number of 1.7.

There were acoustic fatigue test facilities that could generate sound pressure levels up to 164dB and a large scale tunnel (T-101) with a test section measuring 24m by 14m, supported by the ability to measure simultaneously pressures from some 1,500 tappings distributed around a model and deal with lift forces in excess of 10,000 kg. According to a sign nearby, this tunnel had been used in the development of the Antonov An-10, -12, -22, -24, -72, -124 and -225; the Ilyushin Il-18, -62, -76, -86, -96-300 and -114; and the Tupolev Tu-114, 144, -154 and -204.

From Moscow, the party headed to the Rostov Helicopter Manufacturing Enterprise in Rostov on Don, which was the current manufacturing site for the Mi-26 Halo, having previously built Mi-6, Mi-10 and Mi-24. The internal Tu-154 Aeroflot flight felt somewhat uncomfortable, perhaps due to the total lack of seat allocation; the piling of hand baggage against the entry door; and the fact that some of the passengers walked their dogs onto the aircraft.

In Rostov there was a more relaxed atmosphere among the public on the street. The company was, however, finding it difficult to adjust to life without a five year plan.

At the Rostov plant, there was a feeling of guardedness and secrecy.

We were not shown the final assembly facilities, for example, although there was the opportunity to inspect a brand new Mi-26 that had not yet been registered. US Navy test pilot Lt Cdr Ryan was given the opportunity to fly in this aircraft.

The last leg of the trip took us to Poland and a visit to the PZL factory at Lublin and a discussion with staff at Warsaw University.

There was also a very sobering visit to the wartime concentration / extermination camp at Majdanek, near Lublin. PZL had for many years built the Mil Mi-2 helicopter for civil and military use. Production was continuing alongside development and production of their own designs, the Kania (an upgraded Mi-2) and the Sokol.

The company was also starting development of its own small civil helicopter, the SW4.

This was a fascinating trip and something of a unique opportunity.

Poland felt relaxed and welcoming, Russia on the other hand felt like a pretty scary place. The hotel was serving breakfast vodka, at least to Soviet delegations; there were young men driving BMW 7-series cars; and some signs of food shortages. The hotel public areas were also the stamping ground for a series of stunningly beautiful ladies of the night, seeking to convert their favours into hard currency.

Emerging onto Red Square from within the Kremlin, one of our party was 'mugged' by about a dozen children. Three or four of them grabbed each of his arms, immobilising him and allowing the rest of the troupe to extract everything of value from his pockets. The trip featured Halos and Hoodlums, but it's the hoodlums that stick in the memory.

Above: Mig-21 'gate guardian' at TsAGI, Zhukovsky
Below: An as-yet unregistered Mi-26 prepares for a test flight at Rostov

Above: Mil Mi-34 development prototype undergoing structural tests
Below: A lively discussion of past Kamov projects

Above: A brand new Polish Coastguard PZL Sokol approaches completion
Below: Mil Mi-8 MTV-1 in a high-visibility Arctic colour scheme

Above: Kamov Ka-27 Helix ready for inspection by the visitors
Below: Mil Mi-6 Hook at Tomilino with a test radar installation in the nose

The Ka-27 Helix proved to be both quiet and agile

Above: Lt Cdr Ryan of the US Navy flies a brand new Mi26 Halo at Rostov on Don
Below: Petlyakov Pe-2 Polish Air Force Museum, Warsaw

Above: PZL licence-built Mil Mi-2s waiting for the paint shop
Below: PZL Sokol production at Lublin

Image Index

Part 1 - All You need is Lift

Chapter Six "3 to a Room"

Chapter Seven "Do you want to sit in the left hand seat?"

146 - Above and Below: Concorde Right: The general aviation park on the Terminal side of the airfield with 5 DC-3s, a Beech 18 and numerous light aircraft

147 - The general aviation park on the Terminal side of the airfield with 5 DC-3s, a Beech 18 and numerous light aircraft

148 - Above: A typical Oshkosh air show routine – wing-walking and aerobatics in a 450hp Stearman

Below: Oshkosh is famous for warbirds and immaculate restorations, exemplified by this Mustang

149 - Above N2251D 'Miss Coronado' another superb example of the P-51 Mustang

Below Two Curtis P-40s on the flight line, the sort of rare sight that is almost unique to Oshkosh

150 - Above: A rare and totally immaculate Douglas AD-1 Skyraider typifies the unique attractions of Oshkosh

Below: The Canadian Warbirds Heritage Mustang C-FFUZ

151 - Above: A Grumman F-7F Tigercat

Below: The warbirds parking area with B-29, B-24, B-17 and numerous P-51s and T-28s

Part 2 - Lift is All You Need

152 - Schleicher K13 against a Lasham cloudscape

Chapter Eleven "Going for Solo"

155 - Lasham as seen from a high-performance Schempp Hirth Nimbus 3DT

158 - 2009 at Bicester: solo in a glider for the first time since 1967 and cleared to fly the single seat Schleicher K8b

Chapter Twelve "All Aircraft Bite Fools"

161 - British United Carvair 'Menai Straits' in the General Aviation area at Gatwick

162 - Above: A Dan Air Airspeed Ambassador photographed 'through the fence'

Below: Charrington United Breweries bottle-green Piaggio 166 G-ARUJ

164 - Above: One could often see rare and unusual types at Gatwick, in this case McKinnon Turbo-Goose G-ASXG

Below: The Tiger Club was home of both aerobatic and vintage aircraft; this is the sole surviving Arrow Active

166 - Above: Hiller 12E4 of Bristow Helicopters landing at Redhill

Below: Regular RCAF visitors to Gatwick included the Douglas C-47, Bristol Freighter and Canadair Yukon

167 - Above: The early fleet of British United included this Douglas DC-3, in the maintenance area

Below: Adria Airways - another of the small charter airlines flying the Douglas DC-6 out of Gatwick

168 - A typically diverse selection within the Tiger Club Hangar, A shark-toothed Alaparma Baldo 75 in the company of a Chrislea Super Ace, two Turbulents, an Autocar, a Jodel and a Fox Moth

170 - Above: Among the less-than-familiar airlines to be seen was Ariana Afghan Airlines, in this case operating a Douglas DC-6

Below: British United was a launch customer for the BAC One Eleven

171 - Above: The diminutive Levier Cosmic Wind G-ARUL 'Ballerina' was flown by Neil Williams in the World Aerobatic Championships

Below: Percival Q6 G-AFFD was a long-term resident in the Chelsea College of Aeronautics hangar at Redhill

172 - A rare Procaer F15B Picchio seen outside the maintenance hangars at Gatwick

174 - Above: The one-off Storey TSR3 Wonderplane

Below: A Bristol Freighter still in use with Dan Air

175 - Above: The one-off Storey TSR3 Wonderplane was flown at Redhill sporting a Union Jack colour scheme on its upper surfaces

Below: Zlin 526 Trener G-AWAR landed by Neil Williams in a display of outstanding airmanship after suffering a wing spar failure in flight while practising for the 1970 World Aerobatic Championships

279 - Above: Some survivals from the days of early Alaskan aviation are preserved at the Pioneer Air Museum north of Anchorage

Below: Cargo aircraft of all sorts fly freight to out-lying communities; this is a Douglas C-133 Cargomaster

280 - Above: A surviving Aviation Traders Carvair is an unexpected sight among the many cargo aircraft at Anchorage International Airport

Below: One of a number of Fairchild C-119s on the Anchorage ramp

282 - Above: The surviving Boeing YL-15 on the fringes of Lake Hood

Below: A de Havilland Beaver takes off from Lake Hood floatplane workhorse of the northern skies

283 - Above: Piper Super Cub on truck wheels and tundra tyres at Lake Hood airstrip

Below: Another rare bird at Merrill Field a civilianised Convair L-13

284 - Above: Republic Seabee at Lake Hood airstrip

Below: A Fairchild C-82 parked in front of its later development, the C-119 Packet, at Anchorage International

285 - Above: One of the oldest cargo aircraft at Anchorage was this Curtis C-46 Commando. Its colour scheme suggests that it was previously in Japanese Self Defence Force service.

Below: Reeve Aleutian is a long-standing Alaskan airline. At this time it was operating the L188 Electra on passenger routes

286 - Above: Another unusual aircraft of the Reeve Aleutian fleet is this NAMC YS-11 of Japanese origin

Below: The preserved remains of a Bellanca Pacemaker from the pioneering days

287 - Above: A pre-war Curtis Robin sits on floats alongside Lake Hood

Below: Floatplanes can be seen on nearly every Alaskan lake. This is an Aeronca Sedan

288 - This Grumman Goose sits, awaiting restoration, alongside Lake Hood

Chapter Twenty-Four
"Halos and Hoodlums"

292 - The giant and ungainly Mil Mi-24 in storage

295 - Above: A fearsome-looking Hind-D in the Mil experimental hangar

Below: Mil Mi-24 development aircraft at Tomilino

296 - Above: The insect-like Ka-26 Hoodlum

Below: The sprightly Ka-27 Helix shipboard anti-submarine helicopter

299 - Above: Mig-21 'gate guardian' at TsAGI, Zhukovsky

Below: An as-yet unregistered Mi-26 prepares for a test flight at Rostov

300 - Above: Mil Mi-34 development prototype undergoing structural tests

Below: A lively discussion of past Kamov projects

301 - Above: A brand new Polish Coastguard PZL Sokol approaches completion

Below: Mil Mi-8 MTV-1 in a high-visibility Arctic colour scheme

302 - Above: Kamov Ka-27 Helix ready for inspection by the visitors

Below: Mil Mi-6 Hook at Tomilino with a test radar installation in the nose

303 - The Ka-27 Helix proved to be both quiet and agile

304 - Above: Lt Cdr Ryan of the US Navy flies a brand new Mi26 Halo at Rostov on Don

Below: Petlyakov Pe-2 Polish Air Force Museum, Warsaw

305 - Above: PZL licence-built Mil Mi-2s waiting for the paint shop

Below: PZL Sokol production at Lublin

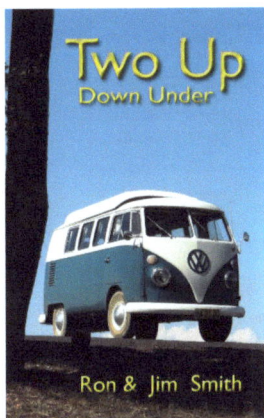

Following on from *Two Up*, in *Two Up Down Under*, Ron and Jim enjoy a road trip around Canberra and the Riverina in Jim's 50-year old VW Kombi, Miss October. As well as the journey, the story of Miss October is told, and, as would be expected, there is a focus on both flying and on vintage aircraft in Australia.

Ron Smith has had a long and varied association with aviation. He is an aerospace engineer, a Fellow of the Royal Aeronautical Society, ex-Chairman of the Royal Aeronautical Society Rotorcraft Committee, author of aviation books and articles, aircraft owner, private pilot and aviation photographer. After 15 years at Westland Helicopters and 22 years with British Aerospace / BAE Systems, Ron's books include the 5 volume *British Built Aircraft* series (The History Press); *Cessna 172: A Pocket History & Piper Cherokee: A Family History* (Amberley Publishing); *Classic Light Aircraft*, & *Twin Cessna*, (Schiffer Publishing).

Jim Smith recently retired from a senior management position after 14 years at the Australian Defence Science and Technology Group. Trained as an aeronautical engineer, he has BSc and Masters degrees from the University of Southampton, UK. Before moving to Australia, Jim worked for the UK Ministry of Defence (MoD) for 28 years. His experience includes involvement with a wealth of British and Australian research and major defence projects, many of which were with international partners.

Paperback ISBN 978-1908135681
Also published as an e-book ISBN 978-1908135698

www.ingramcontent.com/pod-product-compliance
Lightning Source LLC
Chambersburg PA
CBHW040939100426
42812CB00015B/2623